FAT
FREE
MEETINGS

FAT FREE

FREE

MEETINGS

BURT
ALBERT

Peterson's
Princeton, New Jersey

Visit Peterson's at http://www.petersons.com

Library of Congress Cataloging-in-Publication Data

Albert, Burt.
    Fat free meetings / Burt Albert.
      p. cm.
    Includes bibliographical references (p.) and index.
    ISBN 1-56079-597-2
    I. Business meetings—Technological innovations. 2. Communication in management—Technological innovations. I. Title.
    HF5734.5.A42   1996
    658.4'56—dc20
                                    96-41970
                                       CIP

Editorial direction by Carol Hupping
Production supervision by Bernadette Boylan
Copyediting by Katharine Colton
Proofreading by Carol Blumentritt

Composition by Gary Rozmierski
Creative direction by Linda Huber
Interior design by Cynthia Boone

Printed in the United States of America

10 9 8 7 6 5 4 3 2 1

CONTENTS

ACKNOWLEDGMENTS

At General Electric and GTE, I have had the good fortune of working with thousands of employees who have taught me much about what I say in this book. Among the first to spur me on with their intense questions and enthusiasm were those at GE's "Crotonville" and "Nela Park," sites where we explored meeting management in the early stages of Work-Out. To all, hats off!

I'm also indebted to Ken Michel. He launched me into the orbits of both corporations. Wise in the ways of organizational development, Ken deserves a singular niche in the pantheon of the profession. With Pat Scott and Rick Maybury, I've enjoyed countless give-and-takes, not to mention alps of laughs. Close friends and professional colleagues of mine, they're exceedingly generous in their caring and sharing. For that, I can never repay them.

For GTE in particular, I'm limited by space in showering confetti on the many who gave me Ahas! on the task forces we served—worker bees all, despite titles or tenure. But I'd certainly be remiss in not extending special laurels to Julie Phillips, Melitta Lovland, Dave Hinton, and Mary Reiner, "meeting pioneers" within GTE's Telops Information Technology Department.

Carol Hupping, my editor, not only was gracious and judicious but took the hand-off in a relay without breaking stride. What a sprinter! Alan Kellock, gentleman and literary agent, was superb at turning a phrase or two himself, while earning the title Mr. Serendipity. For favors and words of encouragement, I also thank Posey ("Headliner") Griffin and these cherished friends who, over the years, have vicariously ridden the writing road with me: Phil and Tina, Anita and Roland, Dale and BG.

To Heather and Kelley ("How's it going, Dad?") and to my "new son" and advance man, Mike, I'm glad you guys didn't reverse the charges. Seriously though, your calls did do wonders for my batteries. Jewels you are!

Finally, love and hugs to my stellar wife, Lois. "She's as patient as a saint," my Irish aunt would have said. After all, who would have sat at lunch day after day, listening to "my newly minted, priceless prose" and suggesting—in tender tones, each time at the right place—"Why don't you get rid of that?" She's a woman of courage, too, you see. Lucky you! Lucky me!

INTERVIEWEES

Nutmeg and cinnamon. Tarragon. A dash of paprika. Those spices and more—in the form of interview excerpts—add zest to *Fat Free Meetings*. Representing nineteen distinctive voices from an assortment of occupations, as well as organizations varying in size, type, and location, the interviewees cited below offer provocative insights and helpful tips. To each I also owe a toast of thanks: *salud!*

In positions as demanding as yours or mine—and some decidedly more so—these leaders depend on well-run, productive meetings to accomplish as much as they do. Their comments are sure to perk up your taste buds and give you food for thought. Savor and enjoy.

ROSTER OF INTERVIEWEES

Col. Kenneth D. Cameron
Astronaut
NASA, Johnson Space Center
Houston, TX

Page Ayres Cowley and Scott
   Duenow
Partners
Page Ayres Cowley Associates,
   Architects, Llp
New York, NY

Bill Delmont
Vice President
Director of Sales (National and
   International)
UPS
Atlanta, GA

Frank. R. Finch, P.E.
President
Search Technologies
Subsidiary of Geo-Centers, Inc.
Newton Centre, MA

John F. Howell
President and CEO
Easter Seal Society of Hawaii
Honolulu, HI

James J. Knoska
President, Health Systems
Baxter Healthcare Corporation
Deerfield, IL

Suzanne La Rosa
Publisher
Threads magazine and books
The Tauton Press
Newtown, CT

Richard C. Maybury
President
Peak Performance Group
Gloucester, MA

Gordon Nelson
Program Manager
Corporate Leadership Development
General Electric Co.
Fairfield, CT

Julie Phillips
Technology Architect, Strategy and
   Technology Planning
GTE Telephone Operations
Tampa, FL

acknowledgments

Tannia Peeples
Vice President, Human Resources
Time Customer Service
Tampa, FL

William A. Schaffer
Business Services Manager, Europe
Sunsoft, Inc.
Subsidiary of Sun Microsystems
Mountainview, CA

John Sundy, M.D., Ph.D.
Fellow in Rheumotology, Allergy, and
   Clinical Immunology
Duke University Medical Center
Durham, NC

Myrna Walton
Director of Program Coordination,
   UC Benefits
University of California
Office of the President
Oakland, CA

Charles B. Wang
Chairman and CEO
Computer Associates International,
   Inc.
Islandia, NY

Patricia Wunderlin
Vice President
Bay Consulting of Tampa
Tampa, FL

Barbara Metzger
Audioconference Facilitator
Communication Development
   Corporation
Danbury, CT

Patrick Y. Yang, Ph.D.
Vice President, Procurement and
   Materials Management
Merck & Co., Inc.
Whitehouse Station, NJ

part I

REDUCING LIQUIDS

"This process is used mainly to intensify flavor: a wine, a broth, or a sauce is evaporated and condensed over lively heat. A so-called double consommé is made in this way, the final product being half the original in volume."

Joy of Cooking

1 | *crossfire* looked like a tea party!

The need for streamlining meetings in a customer-demanding age

"**Where's** your armor?" he asked me. "By now I had expected to hear the clanking of sword, the roar of cannon." His half-drawn smile burst into a thunder of laughter.

Paul knew that meetings on the topic—the source of a technology holy war—had been called dozens of times during the previous three years. But each get-together had ended in a shouting match that made TV's *Crossfire* look like a tea party!

In fact, for the meeting of the task force to which Paul referred, the dozen members initially acted as if they had been assigned to a congressional subcommittee on the abolition of Mother's Day. No one, and I mean no one, wanted to be tainted by the topic—until word of progress and civil discourse leaked from the room. Then phones began to ring, and e-mails cluttered the computer screens.

Everyone, it seemed, was clamoring to join the group. Because its multimillion-dollar decision would help set the company's course for the twenty-first century, many wanted to have their say. No longer could they seek comfort and job security in lard-laden, decision-evasive meetings. For the sessions of this three-week, intensive undertaking would prove to be not only successful but fat-free; free of the time-wasting, costly behaviors and attitudes that weigh most meetings down and doom them from the beginning:

- *free of* turf battles that leave the customer wanting
- *free of* the silo-thinking that ignores the forces driving a business
- *free of* topical agendas not worth a plugged nickel
- *free of* an almost total reliance on the spoken word
- *free of* conjecture about expectations and deliverables
- *free of* delays and digressions
- *free of* interrupted or irregular attendance
- *free of* distrust and finger-pointing
- *free of* perplexed or unprepared participants
- *free of* withheld information
- *free of* troublemakers—from Mute to Motor Mouth
- *free of* the recurring quick fixes and pseudo-decisions that do nothing more than aggravate the pains of meeting sclerosis

In the end, the holy war combatants became compatriots. The hills and valleys they had crossed—at times in the heat of impassioned debate—faded in the glow of victory for all, especially the company's customers.

Now, with this book, you can enjoy the same kinds of success with the same streamlining, team-building meeting techniques. Whether you're involved with task forces, spur-of-the-moment get-togethers, or other types of powwows (and who isn't?), you too can make them fat free. What's more, in these slim-trim, competitive times, you *must*. You have no other choice: Your organization depends on it.

IMMEDIATE NEEDS ARE CRUCIAL

Meetings are at the heart of virtually everything we do in business, as ideas have become the "new products" in a knowledge industry churning with change.

In meetings we make the discoveries and decisions that speed products and services to market, outwit the competition, and improve the bottom line. If a company ignores the importance and centrality of meetings in conducting business—and lets them lumber in lethargy—it will be choked by inefficiencies, lose talent and potential revenues, and even court failure. Here's why:

- Customers are sophisticated, impatient, and hard to please. They want results *now!*—not to mention quality and reliability. Research by George Stalk and Tom Hout of the Boston Consulting Group suggests, however, that "more than 95 percent of in-house activities (including meetings and the swapping of memos and e-mails) add little value in terms of the deliverables that make a difference to a customer." Making that difference ought to be the focus in meetings—a focus as pinpointed as a laser beam, even when the customer is internal.

> "Netscape is like a rocket. If it fails to reach escape velocity, it will crash back to earth. We've gotta go full speed."
>
> *Jim Barksdale*
> *CEO, Netscape*
> *Communications*

- Acquisitions and mergers are thrusting together employees who are virtual strangers from different business cultures—as well as different races and ethnic groups—but who are often left to figure out for themselves how to work together. Meetings, which should become the primary vehicles for assimilation and cooperation, just keep putt-putting about like Model Ts.

- Dissatisfied customers scoot elsewhere, pouring revenues into the pockets of competitors. They've often been ticked off by interdepartmental squabbles, indecisiveness, or other delays in the meetings of the companies they abandoned. What's more, 91 percent never return.

    Even charities, churches, and other nonprofit organizations run into meeting-related problems as they try to hold on to a diminishing number of volunteers—such as my wife. Upon returning from a meeting last week, she clenched her teeth and said, "If I have to go through another two hours like that, I'm heading for the inactive list."

- The days of the slap-on-the-back order-takers have gone the way of spats and bustles. Long-term alliances are undergirded by the quality of the give-and-take with which they're cemented. No longer can a supplier afford to run meetings, including face-to-face sales calls, with all the finesse of a sumi wrestler partnering a ballerina.

- Landing the Big Deals is more and more dependent on successfully selling colleagues, suppliers, and others. Without their knowledge and input on projects often complicated and months long, humongous sums are jeopardized. "If an organization isn't generating new ideas," writes psychologist Tom McDonald in *Successful Meetings*, "it's only shuffling old ones around. And in a climate that values knowledge, that bureaucratic behavior is the death knell of any business."

    Such concern undoubtedly lies behind the rise of teams in nearly 73 percent of U.S. businesses, while in Fortune 500 companies, work teams consisting of members from different sites have risen to 89 percent. Yet recent accounts tell of groups foundering and failing. Like houses built on sand, they often lack strength in the fundamentals of meeting management. After all, as Coleman Finkel, president of the Conference Center Development Corporation, points out, "most managers have absolutely no training in the skill."

> "Soft skills are every bit as important to a pilot as the knowledge of how the hydraulic system works."
>
> *Captain Pete Wolfe*
> *Southwest Airlines*

TECHNOLOGY: PLAYING CATCH-UP

Pretty scary, isn't it? Even scarier when you consider how technology is changing the face of the workplace and the way business is conducted.

Just think: If employees are already handicapped in the "basics of meetings"—and many are severely so—how in heaven's name will they be able to use the collaborative tools of tomorrow to maximize productivity when they haven't yet learned to exploit the tools of today?

What good will it be to have modems and electronic copyboards (is yours working?), desktop videoconferencing, groupware, or other gee-whiz devices if employees are still mucking about in the dinosaur days and ways of communication? The propensity for going off on tangents, confused priorities, ill-prepared participants, and the forgotten customer are not automatically remedied by the wizardry of an electronic world. *Group grope is group grope, no matter if it occurs on an international video hookup or across a conference table.*

That's why *Fat Free Meetings* starts where most employees are, not in some sci-fi officeland. It provides a transition, taking people who are neither meeting masters nor clones of Bill Gates and easing them into tomorrow.

The Great White-Collar Crime

It doesn't take a brain surgeon to figure out that the need for improving meetings grows more urgent by the day, by the hour. Not just because of aspirin-popping and stressed-induced absences. Not just because the world is indeed a global village and can be spanned within a nanosecond. Not just because networks of telecommuters (some 25 million by the year 2000) and outsource vendors are skyrocketing in number. And not just because most employees spend between 50 and 80 percent of their time in meetings—nearly half or more of their work lives!

Those issues notwithstanding, the most pressing reasons to focus on better meeting management are the need to reduce waste and improve productivity.

Industry Week has referred to the $37 billion wasted annually on meetings as "the great white-collar crime," while the 3M Meeting Management Institute reports that "training in how to manage meetings can increase overall productivity by 58 percent and reduce meeting time by 28 percent." Yet it can be a Herculean task to convince some top-ranking executives, especially comptrollers, that investing in the training of meeting management will deliver significant payback. "Too soft a skill," they squawk. "It can't be measured."

HOWELL: I know a comptroller who does something better than anyone I have ever seen in my life: He can say "No" to anything. But the problem is I never hear him say "Yes." He's not a risk-taker. He has to learn that leadership calls for understanding when to take a person's idea and move with it.

Profitability: Heeding Einstein and Deming

The ledger-keepers fail to heed the admonition Einstein scribbled on the blackboard of his Princeton office: "Not everything counts that can be counted, and not everything that can be counted counts." The words of the genius offer reason enough to say to the cynics or skeptics:

- *Consider the cost* of customers who are not served well because employees are either trapped in meetings or phoning on the run from one crisis to another.

- *Consider the cost* not only of the "30 percent to 50 percent of [the] meetings that fail from lack of objectives" but also the get-togethers where one-fourth of the participants say they discuss irrelevant issues 11 to 25 percent of the time or more, and a third feel they have little or no influence on the outcomes anyway.

- *Consider the cost* of negative spinoffs, such as the gossiping and clarifying that occur after a muddled meeting, the gripe sessions around the water cooler, or the more deliberate forms of employee resistance that, in the United States alone, amount to "$170 billion annually—12 percent of the payroll."

- *Consider the cost* of teleconferences, which are growing "at a 21 percent annual clip since 1989," yet about which a frustrated client recently observed, "A problem occurs and we immediately put all possible participants on a [telephone] bridge and hope they figure it out. The conference goes on for days!"

Similar laments reflecting the dismal state of meeting management should also prod us to:

- *Consider the cost* of technology installed but barely exploited to benefit collaboration.

CAMERON: If I were better with some of those fancy tools (touted for meetings and presentations), I'd use them. But the learning curve with some is so high that I prefer to get an idea on a piece of paper quickly and see what somebody thinks of it.

- *Consider the cost* of JIC-Ps (jick peas), the Just-in-Case Persons who, unaware of what is likely to happen in a meeting or why it's being called, attend to cover their butts—just in case something pertinent pops up. With companies reorganizing on an average of every 18 months, roles and responsibilities keep shifting. Hence, JIC-Ps abound.

- *Consider the cost* of documents gathering dust on office shelves or devouring googols of gigabytes online. From strat plans and marketing plans to user guides and request for proposals (RFPs), as well as policies, practices, and procedures, most of the documents represent a gazillion meetings and gobs of wasted hours, not to mention an incoherence betraying the group grope that produced the mountains of mush. No wonder people find meetings more painful than root canal.

DELMONT: We happen to believe meetings are very necessary—critical to communicating company mission and objectives. That is not to say we don't try to put a price on them, to question the number of meetings and their frequency.

The companies fumbling around in this economy and particular era don't know how to articulate the message to the rank and file. If you tell the people in an organization what to do and the *reasons* you want to do it, they'll go do it. The problem is, they get mixed signals and mixed messages and don't know what to do. That's what's happening—and why we value meetings.

On the other hand, when the tortures are eliminated and meetings become slim-trimmed by a let's-give-it-a-go, results-oriented attitude, employees are more likely to work with energy and synergy, creativity, and curiosity, as well as a desire to go the extra mile, even without the boss's prods and praises. Such outcomes represent the kinds of unknowns and unknowables referred to by W. Edwards Deming, the father of Total Quality Management. Heeding them, said one of his disciples recently, "is ten times more important to profitability than any short-term accounting measure you can quantify."

KNOSKA: I tell 'em, "Hey, we're in this together. In the end we're only one company, one stock price."

---

2 faster than fruit flies

What causes meetingmania, and how well-run meetings can serve as instruments of organizational change

The costs of meetingmania, as you've just seen, are astronomical. Some might even call poorly run meetings cancers on the backs of organizations that must be rooted out at their very source.

CAUSES OF MEETINGMANIA

Two pervasive causes of meeting frenzy are:

• **The transparency of meetings.** Though meetings are the engines that drive a business and provide a platform for detecting high-potential employees, they get less attention than the lobby's potted plants. The latter, you see, are more likely to show up on a ledger.

Recently, for instance, I asked Lauri if she was planning to do anything about meeting management in the curriculum for new hires at a Fortune 50 corporation. Her answer? "No, I'm going to focus on listening and negotiating"—as if those skills occurred in a vacuum. She failed to see the connections, the context.

- **Failure to ask or understand why.** When people don't know *why* they're doing *what* they're doing, they just keep doing, doing, doing, often holding meeting after meeting after meeting.

    Though reengineering tried to address the pivotal questions—*why* are we doing it? *where* is the added value?—I still see ample evidence of antiquated practices and procedures breeding the meetings that barnacle many an organization. Though the beacons of vision and mission statements are out there, the words are fogbound.

    Even the designs of organizations, such as the two that follow, can affect the abundance of meetings:

- **Rigid organizational structure.** In companies where fear reigns and a hierarchy is firmly in place, meetings and memos are the primary vehicles for conducting business—the more the better, hoping to reassure a curmudgeonly CEO that all is well.

    Particularly in this kind of environment, firefighting—holding quick-fix meetings to address problems that will inevitably flare up again—appeals to the macho managerial squadrons that get few thrills from fire prevention. Besides, the more flare-ups attended, the more chevrons from the chief.

- **A highly fluid, participatory structure.** With downsizing, some organizations have become loose, sporadically changing their structures. Employees, told they've been empowered, are often confused by what the term really means and by roles and responsibilities that seem to shift with the tide. So meetings become mechanisms for keeping up-to-date with changes—who's doing what for whom, when, and where—instead of accommodating the business drivers or satisfying the customer's wants and needs.

    Matters of trust, teaming, and technology also contribute to the mania, as evidenced by:

- **The curse of more.** The minute a company survey reveals a low score in the category of "employee trust"—a common occurrence these days—panic spreads: "We need more communication." Not *better*, you notice, but *more*. Without taking time to determine what observable behaviors underlie the lack of trust, the powers that be and all their factotums offer *more* publications, *more* pronouncements, *more* powwows!

- **The hydra-headed monsters.** With the increase in teams of all sizes and species, meetings have sprung up like hydra-headed monsters, be they gatherings of subcommittees, focus groups, or other delegated offshoots. Without expiration dates or a clear sense of their mandates, the new creatures take on lives of their own. And—horror of horrors!—some reproduce faster than fruit flies.

- **The need for touch.** The increase in technology, says Patricia Aburdeen, co-author of *Megatrends 2000*, will increase face-to-face get-togethers. "The more technology you have in your office and at your house," she points out, "the more you need to balance that with the high touch of the personal meeting."

Finally, language and techniques of communication exacerbate the problem in ways not always recognized or appreciated. Some examples:

- **"Gossip" mongers.** It's easier to talk it than write it. That seemingly universal attitude feeds meeting overload.

  Remember: The spoken word goes POOF! And if meeting attendees have not delivered the precise meanings they intended to deliver in their seltzer bubbles of talk, or they have not listened well, or they leave the meeting without common understandings agreed to and recorded, then the meeting has been nothing more than a variation on the game of "Gossip."

  In some schools, the game still substitutes for recess on a rainy day. Sue writes a sentence on a slip of paper and whispers it to Danny in the seat behind her. Danny then whispers the message to Melanie, who in turn passes it on to Lou, and so on. At the end of the cycle the last kid says aloud what she or he has just heard, which invariably bears little or no resemblance to the original sentence Sue announces. The class howls with laughter.

  It's no laughing matter in business, however, where the pattern of the old game leaves too much at stake, particularly in the spinoff meetings that grow exponentially as participants try to clarify what was said in preceding get-togethers or to act on the recollections of meeting amnesiacs.

- **Knee-jerk reactions.** Too often meetings are called on impulse—to please a demanding superior, prop up a bumbling boss, oblige a firefighting customer. No matter their source, however, all are whipped up by words—what they mean to the sender, to the receiver.

Without stopping to question such words—be they mindbenders or said impetuously perhaps—eager-to-please, puzzled, or angry receivers call meetings of one sort or another: "Help! The customer wants it and wants it now!" "What do you think *this* means?" "I'll show *you* a thing or two!" And with companies whirring like Cuisinarts, hastily spoken or written words become part of the swirl—chopped, mangled, and minced. Too many cooks get involved, and the groaning boards of meetings grow legion.

- **One-way messaging.** Instead of questioning and probing an issue collaboratively, meeting participants often prefer one-way transmittals of information in which egospeak predominates. The emphasis is more on "Notice me. Here's what *I* have to say" than "How can I be assured you understand the precise meaning I'm trying to convey?"

  "Collaboration," says Michael Schrage of MIT, "is the process of *shared creation*: two or more individuals with complementary skills interacting to create a shared understanding that none had previously possessed or could have come to on their own."

  "In practice," Schrage contends, "collaboration is a far richer process than teamwork's handing off on an idea or blocking and tackling for a new-product rollout or attempting a slam-dunk marketing maneuver. The issue isn't communication or teamwork—it's the creation of value . . . a process that our traditional structures of communication and teamwork can't achieve."

  Failing to recognize such distinctions can, of course, brew stews of meetings. Without really knowing it, participants struggle to make a discovery—the Aha! of a *shared understanding*—simply by exchanging stories of their own individual experiences. It's inefficient. And it rarely works.

- **Worship of the coin.** In corporate America, attention is riveted on the bottom line. Forgotten is the Biblical pronouncement "In the beginning was the word." It's not "In the beginning was the coin" or "the microchip," or "the fiberoptic cable." The *word* is the bottom line.

  When a company's representative in Hong Kong wants information immediately from headquarters in Boston and from a Chicago supplier, what good are the laptops and faxes if the messages they transmit are too brief or unclear about the expected actions of the three sites? Such ambiguities, which are common, lead to electronic conversations attempting to clarify an original message. The resulting delays—even of a few minutes—can make the difference between landing a customer and losing one.

No matter our titles or positions, we are all managers of conversations and commitments, the fundamentals of which are language. And whether words are spoken or written, it is how well we use them—how clearly and concisely, effectively and efficiently—that determines not only the financial profits we enjoy but, ultimately, their magnitude.

MEETINGS: INSTRUMENTS OF CHANGE

Isn't it strange? Companies pour cargoes of money into teaching employees how to conduct business in other lands and cultures but do little to encourage employees to learn about the subcultures within their own organizations.

In upstate New York, for example, I had a client company in which the data processing people spoke quite a different language from those in finance. Beyond terminology, chasms also existed in how each department ran, what they thought the business was, and who their customers were perceived to be. Such divergences, if left unanswered, had affected meetings in all kinds of counterproductive ways.

NELSON: We tend to minimize the importance of recognizing subcultures within a business. If manufacturing minimizes the importance of engineering and engineering minimizes the importance of manufacturing, then it's difficult for them to get together, to communicate.

At another company, in a course for employees from a cross-section of technologies, a program manager chose to devote two hours of the first day not to a session on the organizational subcultures represented by the group of virtual strangers—something that was never done—but to a wine steward offering instruction in the fine art of ordering and pouring. "We have to be sure our folks know this stuff," said an assistant, with neither tic nor twit. "For you can never tell where they may have to go in these days of globalization."

And speaking of training, look at the discrete courses on leadership, teamwork, internal customer service, supervision, and a catalog of other related topics. *Most, if not all, are taught outside the context of meeting management.*

In fact, the index of a well-known text on supervision, now in its sixth edition, lists only a single page devoted to meetings. Yet, because meetings are at the heart of disparate communities working within a company, they provide excellent opportunities for effecting organizational change, especially when there's a uniform and consistent attitude about the way meetings are run—from boardroom to workroom.

KNOSKA: Someone in a meeting *has* to be the customer advocate. If everybody is thinking myopically and not thinking about where the bread is buttered, the customer is not going to be involved. To be successful you have to *think* like the customer.

What better place for leaders to demonstrate how they can walk the talk, inspire others, listen carefully, achieve alignment, and so on. For participants, meetings can become settings where the role-play of the classroom is tested in real life by the authenticity of transactions, including cross-functional/cultural teaming and conflict resolution. Most important, when the business and customer take center stage in such meetings, the subcultures begin to realize why barriers must tumble to serve what's common to their bond.

3 instant shrinkers

Starting a meeting meltdown—right now!—with 20 hot tips

In a world where we nuke our meals in microwaves and twit the post office for "snail mail," we've grown impatient with anything not instant. Hence this chapter. It offers tips on how you can begin streamlining meetings immediately. There are also a few suggestions about agendas and sketches, which lay the groundwork for detailed explanations later on.

Though most suggestions are given from a leader's perspective, don't hesitate to run with an idea as a committee member: Thinking the person who called the meeting is solely responsible for its success is one of the biggest fat-adders around. Kill the thought—right now, this instant!

Pack a grab-and-go meeting kit. Buy yourself an oversize legal folder, an inexpensive artist's portfolio, or a portable file cabinet. Stock it with these basics and add to it as you discover other handy devices:

- a pad of self-adhesive easel sheets
- an oversize sketch pad or pad of newsprint
- an oversize pad of tracing paper
- a lightweight wall clock with batteries
- markers in assorted colors
- write-on transparencies
- masking tape
- transparency markers
- pushpins
- 3 × 5 and 5 × 8 index cards
- magnetic clips

Whenever you have to dash to a meeting—whether you've called it or someone else has—grab the kit. You'll be surprised by the ways these items stimulate the time-saving and important language of sketching (see Don't Just Chew the Fat, later in this chapter).

Also, the tools will encourage people to use walls for either postings or storyboards of index cards and, if necessary, metal chair backs for display. Participants might even blow the dust off an overhead projector or, for the lack of a projector, substitute sheets from the tracing pad as flimsies and overlays. In short, the tools will help control—more importantly, diminish—ad hoc powwows and the seltzer bubbles of talk.

Put a face in the place. Install a clock in every meeting room. If that can't be done, take the timepiece from your grab-and-go kit and hang it on a pushpin. A clock face—especially one with big black dials and a sweeping second hand—keeps attendees from succumbing to open-ended meetings and Parkinson's Law: *Work expands so as to fill the time available for its completion.*

METZGER: Starting a teleconference on time is more critical than in a live meeting because holding on a phone can seem forever. Our company works and bills minute to minute, so every one is critical.

With hand and dials circling in front of them, meeting members become more concise, more sensitive to the relevance of topics raised. If someone does go off on a tangent, it's easier for a leader or a participant to yank the meeting back on track; the clock can become "the heavy." What's more, a prominent clock gives you a vehicle for speeding the meeting with comments such as these:

- *We've set 15 minutes for the first item. That means a wrap-up by 9:10. You're on, Andy.*
- *The next item might give us a chance to play catch-up. We allotted 20 minutes, but perhaps we can get done by 9:35.*
- *Great job, Loni. Your preso was a testament to the old adage: Be bright, be brief, be gone. Thanks to you we're back on schedule.*

Judgment, of course, must come to bear. If deliberation is helpful and running full throttle, give an item the extra time it deserves or suggest carry-over to the next meeting. Work first and hardest, however, on training participants to say what they have to say in the most economical way.

STAND FOURSQUARE

C'mon now. Be honest. Do you really need that get-together after all?

Take the "Twinge Test." Before calling a meeting, stand foursquare at the mirror of truth. Ask yourself the questions below. If a guilty conscience makes you twinge or the glass cracks, think twice or thrice before calling and hauling people from their work:

- *What headline would I want to see come out of the meeting?*
- *Would the news be something the customer was happy to have paid for?*
- *What will participants take away from the meeting? What will its value be?*
- *In a criminal context, could the meeting be construed as violating any law pertaining to kidnapping or grand larceny?*
- *Will the meeting deal with a practice, procedure, or other matter that should have gone the way of the hula hoop?*
- *How will I measure the success of the meeting? That is, what specific things will I see or hear?*
- *What would happen if I didn't call the gathering?*

Steer clear of scapegoats and Rambo camouflage. Complete this sentence: *The purpose of the meeting is to . . . .* If you find yourself slack-jawed and saying "Duh" because you're not clear about what you want to accomplish, stop! Abort the thought of meeting. Suspect your motives whenever you're planning to:

- attempt a quick fix
- prolong decision making until a scapegoat stumbles onto the scene
- give more attention to a matter than it deserves
- ignore or violate this time-management principle: The important is seldom urgent; the urgent is seldom important
- do anything that doesn't directly or indirectly accommodate the client or the business drivers
- plan a meeting for the meeting of the meeting
- avoid writing about an issue that demands the weighing of words

Also think otherwise if you intend to:

- give a customer, co-worker, boss, or supplier the illusion that all is well
- cater to your preference for communicating by talking, despite participants' preference for reading and reflecting
- avoid one-on-one meetings where vulnerabilities might seem more transparent and self-threatening or where "bad news" might surface more readily
- finger-point, spread blame, or emit a resounding "Harumph!"
- appear "democratic and empowering," although you're known as Rambo
- avoid real, honest-to-goodness, value-added work

NEITHER CHIMP NOR CHUMP

Get the monkey off your back. When it comes to meeting management, share the load, putting much of it where it belongs: on the shoulders of participants.

Squelch sit-downs for updates. Watch the fat melt when attendees, shifting from foot to foot, are quick to make their reports, eager to say "Pass," and restricted to topics concerning the whole group. When collaboration is not the focus, that's how most status-report meetings should be handled. Keep each to 20 minutes or less and have a note-taker record key points either on an overhead transparency that's reproduced and distributed right after the meeting or on a copyboard for instant printouts.

FINCH: I find most folks cannot summarize unless forced to. Whenever I took over a new post, I often found I had to interrupt my officers abruptly and leave the room—though it was painful for me to do that—to make these points: (1) My time's valuable, and (2) I can't indulge you because you haven't thought about what's important and pared it down to the essentials requested.

Note: Finch, who recently became president of Search Technologies, was interviewed just before he retired as the U.S. Army's Chief Environmental Officer.

Rotate 'em. For each meeting of a team or for a set of consecutive meetings, appoint a different leader. Give the person the opportunity to know what it's like to plan an agenda, to keep a meeting on track, to gain the attention of colleagues who are as animated as fireplugs or think they're cruising the Med. The experience develops leadership skills, of course, while helping to make each member of the group a more empathetic, active, and effective participant.

YANG: I've been rotating meeting leadership for years. The practice can really turn what can be a rather boring mechanism into an exciting experience for all.

MAP A FLIGHT PLAN—WITH TAB!

You wouldn't board a plane without knowing the destination or cost of the trip. Those same concerns should be at the forefront of slenderizing any get-together.

Chart your route. If you're not already doing so, or you've always resisted the idea, work by agenda. Don't balk or squawk. Excuses are verboten.

The lack of an agenda is the number-one meeting ballooner, allowing people to dominate, to carom from one "personal topic" to another, to slog in the bogs of irrelevancies, to revisit issues, to get little or nothing done. As a first step to a lean and clean get-together, make sure you have an agenda with time allotments that look like this (10:00-10:15) instead of this (15 minutes). Then, heeding the suggestions in this book, do all you can to stick to the agenda. Plan your work, work your plan.

COWLEY: We prefer to work by agenda. It keeps people focused and prevents them from going off into gossip. Even with a client who trusts and adores us, we try to keep some kind of paper trail. I believe it strengthens our relationship.

LA ROSA: Between the alpha and omega of a meeting, participants need to have a sense of what they're being asked to contribute.

Exercise the slim-trimmer. Urge committee members to fill out a form or online template similar to the one on page 21 when submitting an agenda item for an upcoming meeting:

By completing the form, individuals make these kinds of fat-battling discoveries:

- *This topic would be a waste of the group's time. It's unimportant.*
- *I don't need to bother the whole group with this; I only need to touch base with Marty and Rachel.*
- *Hmm. . . . I'm not really sure what the benefits are. I'd better postpone this topic for now . . . maybe scrap it altogether.*
- *Yeah, I have to fess up; it's only my petty concern. I'll let it pass.*
- *This would probably be handled better in a one-on-one with Tim, our team leader. No reason to rope in the whole gang.*

At times, of course, individuals also find themselves thinking: *I'm more convinced than ever the matter needs to be lifted up. But after seeing the potential benefits, I can now explain and defend my viewpoint in just a few words.*

Discuss the form and its intent with your group so it doesn't inhibit anyone from putting topics on the table that require the members' deliberation. Likewise, agree on the criteria (chop! chop!) that determine which agenda items come to the committee, task force, or other group. Applying the criteria keeps many a meeting menu from spreading into a smorgasbord—a delight only to the gluttons for punishment.

PROPOSED AGENDA ITEM
(BLANK FORM)

1. I Would Like Our Team To:
   (Begin item with a precise, active verb.
   Note: Do not use discuss, review, or a synonym for either word.)

   _____

2. Here Is Why the Item Has Surfaced:

   (Give a concise explanation that provides members with a context for understanding.)

   _____

   _____

3. By Dealing with the Item I/We Will Be Able To:

   (Cite two or three benefits, beginning each with an active verb.)

   • _____

   • _____

4. I Estimate the Item Will Take _____ Minutes.

On page 22 is a completed form. Once your team becomes adept with the tool, you may only need to sequence, reproduce, staple, and distribute the forms for a quickly assembled, informative agenda.

Chalk up the bucks. Each time you call a meeting, calculate its approximate cost—for businesses, conservatively $150 an hour per manager, including overhead—and display the total prominently on the agenda. Remind the group of the cost when you open the meeting and restate its objective(s). At the end, leave time to assess the results against these yardsticks:

• *Would our customers and stockholders have considered this meeting a good return on the investment? Why or why not?*
• *Could we have put the same amount of money to a better use? If so, what might that have been, and is there anything we can still do about it?*

PROPOSED AGENDA ITEM
(COMPLETED FORM)

1. I Would Like Our Team To:
   Approve for the Users' Roundtable the position paper on software.

2. Here Is Why the Item Has Surfaced:
   The addendum, which grew out of a focus group last month, makes suggestions that need immediate attention. What's more, the AVPs have been eager to see more aggressive movement on this front.

3. By Dealing with the Item We Will Be Able To:

   - purchase recommended software at a discount of nearly 30 percent

   - help the training department begin development of a self-paced program to be completed by 4Q.

4. I Estimate the Item Will Take 25 Minutes.

DON'T JUST CHEW THE FAT

Most meetings are larded with yackety-yak. Cut the slack by encouraging people to stop, look, and listen.

Slash an amazing 28 percent! Unless your meeting room is equipped with sophisticated technology, you may still be working with an overhead projector. If that's the case, don't limit transparencies to dog-and-pony shows. Use them in briefings, status-report meetings, virtually every type of get-together. Keep a supply handy at all times for writing on the spot. Visuals help counterbalance the evanescence of the spoken word. They force presenters to think ahead and clarify their own understandings. In short, they help weed out those who have to say something from those who have something to say.

A particularly memorable instance occurred a few years ago during a meeting I audited at a biomedical laboratory near Bethesda, Maryland. I squirmed as a dozen or so Ph.D.s rambled on and on in a room without a clock, each delivering a monologue that seemed longer than a Fidel Castro speech. Finally, a lab colleague grabbed his group's attention with a single transparency of "bullet points." He followed the K.I.S.S. formula—Keep It Simple, Stupid—and wowed them with a message that was not only concise but substantive.

His behavior bore out a study at the University of Pennsylvania's Wharton Research Center. In examining the effects of transparencies on business meeting presentations, researchers concluded:

- Meetings in which transparencies were used ran shorter by 28 percent.
- Less time was spent on lengthy monologues.
- Group decisions were reached more quickly.
- The presenters were viewed as more professional, better prepared, and more persuasive.

So, quick! Take advantage of all those benefits, not the least of which is a nearly 30 percent time reduction. That's a hefty heap of fat!

Appeal to the Picassos. Encourage meeting members to illustrate a point with a sketch—on an easel, copyboard, or overhead flimsy—or with an anecdote, a comparison, or a scenario that helps listeners quickly grasp ideas they might otherwise take hours and hours to "get."

Showing rather than telling is a chief ingredient of a speedy, fat-free meeting. For years I've used the following spurs to make meetings gallop along:

> "To explain himself, [General Electric's CEO, Jack] Welch will hastily sketch chart after chart on a pad of paper, often while eating raw carrots or chewing five sticks of gum at once."
>
> *Noel Tichy and Stratford Sherman*
> Control Your Destiny or Someone Else Will

- *Can you draw us a picture?*
- *Would you please give us an example?*
- *It's hard for most of the group to visualize. See if you can sketch something on the overhead to give us a clearer idea.*
- *You've said there've been a number of problems with that model. What exactly are they? Show us, please.*
- *Perhaps you could describe an analogous situation in another type of organization. That might help us see what you're trying to get at.*

- *I'm going to describe a scenario to show what we'd like the customer to expect. Then tell me how your concept would accommodate that scenario.*
- *Here's what happened last week. How might your prototype have prevented that?*

Showing, not telling, also helps speakers avoid or amend cognitive leaps—omitting information with which they are familiar but listeners are not. And by testing a scenario, as suggested above, participants may find potential glitches that cut off the need for further debate, or they may find reassurance in a tangible depiction that excessive talk—not to mention meanderings—might have made difficult to grasp.

WATCH YOUR WORDS

Don't assume words are always cheap. Ignoring them can block the arteries of communication and impede progress. Avoid that fate.

Create a peaceable kingdom. Help team members give *whole* rather than *partial* messages. As Richard C. Maybury of Peak Performance Group points out, "The English language is built on *polar terms.*" He asks, "What are the midpoints when you try to place a term between *good* and *bad, generous* and *stingy, polite* and *rude, success* and *failure?*"

The "polar" bears of communication tend to roar and rumble in absolutes; it's either black or white. The "gray" squirrels see alternatives. They deal in shades of gray and are likely to accept them when alternatives are supported by feelings and perceptions. "With this is mind," says Maybury, "when communicating any message, we must remember to use language that accepts the possibility of non-absolutes and alternatives. *Absolutes raise antagonism and polarize positions.*"

Whole messages consist of four types of statements, or parts, delivered in this sequence: observations (statements of fact), thoughts (inferences/conclusions drawn), feelings, and needs. If a sender omits any one of the four types in delivering a message—especially one dealing with an interpersonal, potentially volatile topic—the receiver may become confused, unconvinced, irritated, or alienated. And in a frenetic business world, where shorthand is often spoken, the likelihood of omission is significant. For example, instead of saying. . .

Well, Chuck, I guess you're going to be late on the Verucci delivery.

. . . a more diplomatic Ellie would slow down, merge the four types of statements, and say something to this effect:

Chuck, around 8:45 this morning I noticed the guys on the loading dock were not packing the truck for the Verucci delivery. Joe was reading the Post, *Bryan was listening to his tapes, and Les was smoking. According to my printout, the trucks have to be out of here by 1:15 this afternoon. The shipment also involves lots of extra padding and stabilizing. (Observation) If Verucci doesn't get the equipment by Thursday—and in perfect condition—(Thought/Inference), I'm afraid we'll lose the Big V account, which is nearly $450,000 in annual revenue. (Feeling) I made a promise to Max Shields, the P.A. at Verucci's, for on-time delivery. I don't want to have to go back on my word and destroy his perception of our company's credibility and dependability. (Need)*

In this message, Ellie doesn't attack anyone personally. She simply relates what she saw in the way of behaviors, what she inferred, and how that input is affecting her feelings and needs. With that kind of complete information to deal with, Chuck is much more apt to accommodate Ellie than get defensive and berate her.

In meetings, whole messages may take slightly longer to relay, but they save on the buildup of attacks and counterattacks, electronic scuttlebutt, conscious or unconscious resistance, and so on—what Deming would have lumped into the "unknowns and unknowables" affecting profitability.

In your meeting rooms, post the questions on page 26 from time to time. And whenever individuals struggle to make sense of an issue—to create a shared understanding—remind them to send whole messages by answering the questions in the sequence given. Encourage colleagues to do the same with each other. The technique, for the "polar" bears as well as the "gray" squirrels, helps achieve a peaceable kingdom.

Become a neon myna bird. Most unnecessary meetings spring from miscommunications. You can help reduce their number with a couple of simple tools

---

DELIVER A "WHOLE MESSAGE"

1. What facts do you know based on what you actually saw, heard, or read?

2. What inferences or conclusions do you draw from the facts?

3. How do the inferences or conclusions make you feel (without blaming or judging anyone)?

4. What needs do you now have (without blaming or judging) because of the information you related above?

---

that won't cost a cent but will save you plenty. The first is this sentence: *Why do you say that?* And the second is this confirming statement: *Here's what I heard you say.*

When someone makes a sweeping generalization, a comment based on shaky assumptions, or a remark that seems skeptical, negative, puzzling, or otherwise disturbing, ease into seeking an explanation by saying: *That's an interesting viewpoint. Why do you say that?* Or wonder out loud, *Gee! That's a completely different take on the topic. Why do you feel that way? How did you come to that point of view?* The feedback you get should either clarify the speaker's meaning or help the speaker discover his or her faulty reasoning, inflammatory language, or the like, as you inquire further with the same litany that helps the "polar" bears and "gray" squirrels.

Also, after every major segment of an important conversation—certainly after one that may have rambled or one you're supposed to walk away from with specific understandings, action items, or both—tell your interlocutor *Here's what I heard you say.*

Or vary the statement:

- *Is this what you're saying?*
- *Am I correct in understanding that . . . ?*

If you feel a need to reassure Grump you're not deaf or seeking a brain transplant, tell the *why* of the *what*—the benefit to both you and the speaker:

- *I want to make sure I've understood you. So please correct me if I misheard any of the following points. . . .*

- *To make sure we're both on the same wavelength and I get the assignment right, this is what I've heard.*
- *Please let me summarize what I've heard so far. I want to make sure you get exactly what you're after.*

The speaker hears the replayed message and gains an insight:

- *That's not what I meant. I should have said . . . .*
- *You just made me aware of my assumptions about . . . but I don't have any facts to back me up.*
- *Oh, I see I've used some ambiguous words that have thrown you off.*
- *No, you didn't grasp what I wanted you to hear.*
- *Oops, I neglected to mention something.*
- *Yes, that's exactly what I meant, and it's good to know that someone—for this transactional moment—has understood me. (Won't that melt the heart of Grump!)*

Use the phrasings until they become a natural part of your conversation, until people think of you as a neon sign blinking: *Be clear! Be clear! Give a whole message.* At the slight risk of also being called a myna bird, you'll make others conscious of the need to communicate well. Enlist them in your cause.

Gnarl not. Watch out for abstractions and catch phrases entangling the lines of give-and-take. *Customer satisfaction* and *quality service* won't mean exactly the same thing to you as they will to Reggie or Donna or any other member of your committee. Neither will such phrases as *easier way, greater latitude, more initiative,* and—you guessed it—*empowered employees.* Think, too, of *trust* and *respect, dependability* and *integrity*—words bandied about during performance-appraisal meetings.

FINCH: During Hurricane Iniki [Hawaii, September 11, 1992], one of my infantrymen, in his communications, insisted on referring to "1800 hours Zulu time." I said to him, "Look, the people I'm dealing with don't understand that; put in parentheses 8:00 A.M. local time." The guy was dealing with one audience, I was dealing with another. He was technically correct in "going by the book," but "the book" at that point was not appropriate.

Whenever a get-together depends on people sharing a common understanding of an abstraction or catch phrase, stop to define it. Ask yourselves: *What does it look like? How does it sound?* Or make a concrete list of WHAT IT IS vs. WHAT IT IS NOT. Whichever technique the group chooses, agree on a definition for the duration of the dialogue. Write it down for all to see and reflect on, so the alignment of meaning aligns those at the meeting. Asking *What's the meaning of that?* in the first place prevents time-consuming snags, brickbats, and combat.

DON'T LET THEM SNEAK UP

Like calories in certain beverages, the widespread practices alluded to in the next five suggestions add to the weight of meetings bit by insidious bit. Address them the instant you happen upon them and watch the calorie count plummet.

Avoid the offshoots; heed the doctor. Next time your committee, quality circle, or whatever is on the brink of delegating an assignment to an offshoot group, stop and ask the following questions or appoint a "diet doctor" to monitor the tendency and flag the group at the appropriate time.

- *Are we trying to avoid or delay a decision?*
- *Are we creating a scapegoat?*
- *What exactly do we want the spinoff to accomplish that we can't complete ourselves? What added value lies in the intended outcome?*
- *What would happen if we didn't generate the spinoff? Would the result make much of a difference to the customer? Why or why not?*
- *What less expensive, slim-trim ways might we use to achieve the same objectives?*

Zap ASAP. Bag it, burn it, bury it! Do whatever it takes to get rid of that acronym. "As soon as possible" usually has one of two effects, both potentially negative. If it's become a convention with all the snap of a milk-dunked cookie, people will ignore it altogether or respond to the deadline at *their* convenience. If, however, it's tantamount to a papal bull, they'll convene at once—often beckoning others to their circle—to interpret and obey the edict before suffering the thunderous roars of the awaiting almighty.

Forbidden to use the acronym, a writer is apt to cite a specific date, and then explain the reason for that deadline (the *why* of the *what*)—a prime clue to the priority and scope of a request. Then meetings, exchanges of e-mail, and such are likely to be fewer, more focused, and free of the panic that ensues when every petition is received as a life-or-death entreaty.

Screen the JIC-Ps. Substitute representatives should not be allowed to attend meetings without authority to make decisions. Powerless, they become Just-in-Case Persons.

Neither should such attendees be allowed to leave a meeting without receiving a written summary of "bulleted points," preferably on the spot. (Here's where a copyboard, with its printout capabilities, proves to a be a grizzle-frizzler in more ways than one.) Otherwise, the meeting becomes another variation on the game of "Gossip," in which substitutes report back to the no-shows what they think they heard in the spritz of give-and-take. And their distortions, omissions, and inadvertent additions result in showers of hours to clean up the muck.

Strangle the monsters. Get control of distribution lists. If you're inundated with e-mails, voice messages, or stacks of hard-copy memos with long distribution lists, you already know how the appendages choke an organization like the arms of a giant squid. If not, read on. Realize why the distribution list may be one item that demands a policy or practice. Lobby for it.

Warn of the impending death. Stop issuing reports that head directly for the shredder or the electronic Elysian Fields. Every six months or so, send out an announcement such as the following, repeat it two or three times, and then make decisions based on the responses:

What Do You Say: End It Or Not?

After (date), the report on (title) will no longer be published unless we find sufficient reasons to continue it. We believe its value may have run its course. If you disagree, please tell us no later than (date) why the publication should remain.

If it's important enough to them, readers will take the time to reply. What's more, you may be surprised at what they consider helpful or unhelpful. On the other hand, when you receive issues of a worthless document because you're on a routine or an automated distribution list, purge your name. Send a request such as the following, including the tickler of a postscript to route skimmers back to the basic message:

Purge Me!

Please take my name off the distribution list for (title). Because the information is not appropriate to my work, I hate having you waste time—or paper—on my behalf. I'm sure you'd prefer using both in some other way. Many thanks.

P.S. I'll look forward to *not* receiving this report.

If more people shared such information with those who generate periodic reports, not to mention reports that are unnecessarily long or outdated, the effects would include:

- fewer documents and the meetings attendant to them
- wafer-thin documents better targeted to niches of readers
- time freed for other, more productive tasks. . . especially if you carry out this final suggestion as well:

Bury 'em at Gloryville. On Tuesday morning, Thursday morning, or both, impose a moratorium on meetings held among employees. Or sound the death knell for *all* types of get-togethers during those periods—be they in your department only or throughout the organization. Discover how the moratorium reconfigures your time—and that of others—for more productive ends. Thrill at an epiphany or two about certain meetings that long ago begged for black crepe and a final ditching. In business, those kinds of RIP-offs bring cheers, not tears. Hallelujah! Hallelujah!

4

3 × 5s for the general and me

Using index cards to evade the energy drains of Fat City

During Operation Desert Storm, General William G. "Gus" Pagonis pulled off a record-breaking logistics operation involving "122 million meals served, 1.3 billion gallons of fuel pumped, 52 million miles driven, and 32,000 tons of mail delivered." How did he manage all that? With 20-minute stand-up meetings and 3 × 5 index cards.

Now executive vice president, logistics, for Sears Merchandise Group, Pagonis heads a "6,000-employee operation responsible for shipping about 7 billion pounds of freight a year." In his book, *Moving Mountains: Lessons in Leadership and Logistics from the Gulf War,* the former three-star Army general described his techniques. His use of the 3 × 5 cards intrigued me because I, too, had discovered their streamlining advantages years ago. So I wrote him—on a card, of course—to find out if he had transferred the tool to the private sector. He replied:

31

Yes, I have been using 3 × 5 cards at Sears. It is working great. Also, I use the 3 × 5 format for e-mail. They [i.e., the correspondents] can't exceed the 3 × 5 card format—and this is working well. I get about 50 to 60 [e-mails] a day—short/concise, and very timely information. Also, they are used from the lowest level of the organization (distribution centers to the home office). Bottom line: great management tool that caught on immediately.

The card is such a simple, low-tech device—tangible and portable, efficient and effective, and, best of all, cheap. Besides, its payoffs are incredible: Picture the myriad communications involved in determining, ordering, receiving, and dispensing the ingredients for 122 million individual meals! If a 3 × 5 card can expedite that kind of monumental effort, what could it do for you and your meetings?

Following are several time-tested suggestions on how to use or adapt the cards for that purpose, including tips you can share with participants. Other uses pop up throughout this book.

Although not necessary, it's advantageous to have a desktop copier handy when using cards in a collaborative meeting where people are occasionally polled or invited to write certain kinds of responses. Many times you'll find—once people have become comfortable with each other and aren't afraid to reveal themselves in open debate or through their handwriting—being able to slap sets of cards atop a copier and produce an instant handout speeds matters even more.

To ensure anonymity until everyone is comfortable with each other, you may wish, as appropriate, to collect and read responses aloud. Or make handouts during a break after having someone key in the responses—on a laptop or at a committee-room workstation with a high-speed laser printer. For example, in a brainstorming session, rather than waste time with individual contributions written on a common easel sheet or copyboard, you might have participants jot down their ideas on separate cards, reproduce them on the spot—three cards to a page—and then distribute the copies.

GENERAL 3 × 5 GUIDELINES

For the best results:

1. Be sure stacks of index cards are within reach of every participant. Lined cards are best because the lines keep people from scrawling a single entry when a numbered listing is called for.

2. Have ballpoint pens available for respondents whose pressure on a pencil point has the weight of a cat's whisker. Dark lettering helps reproduction.

3. Tell respondents to work with the cards horizontally, writing on one side only, to speed the reproduction of three cards per page of a handout.

4. Consider these options for expediting feedback:

   - When anonymity is not an issue, ask each person to put her or his name at the top right-hand corner of a card and number the items, so references can consist of "Marybeth's Number 1" "Karl's Number 3" and so on.

   - When people are reluctant to reveal their identities, do not have them number their items for copying, because the cards should be gathered and numbered as one complete lot. Reproduce the lot and give group members a minute or so to number all items consecutively on their individual copies.

FAT-COUNTERING TIPS FOR PARTICIPANTS

Pass on the following suggestions to meeting-goers. They're aimed at preventing behaviors that stop trains of thought, break momentum, or take a meeting off track. The annotations are primarily for your benefit but share them with participants whenever helpful.

Make notes. Prepare to share a thought after another participant has finished making his or her point.

Pass notes to a colleague rather than comment out loud. Minimize whispering and similar distractions while still allowing people to share thoughts—even humorous ones—that might be brought to the group's attention later. Because note-passing is a more conscious act than casually turning to a neighbor and conversing, meeting members tend to exchange notes with discretion, resulting in better listening.

Trap and track Ahas! When someone suddenly gets an idea, she or he should jot it down immediately rather than impulsively interrupt a speaker or depend on short-term memory.

In collaborative get-togethers where posted easel sheets are displayed and entitled ISSUES, TO DO'S, RECOMMENDATIONS, and the like, occasionally a group member will say, "I think that's an issue we need to address" or "I hear a potential recommendation" or "That's a To Do." Rather than stop to log the suggestion in front of the group or try to retain the thought altogether, invite the contributor to note the idea and transfer it to the appropriate sheet during the next break. Later, handle the entries according to whatever steps the group has agreed to, but don't disrupt momentum with a clerical distraction.

Capture action items for yourself, delegatees, or both. The individual 3 × 5 cards make it easier to deal with discrete tasks by allowing you to slot them into an organizer or delegate them later to direct reports. What's more, it is not uncommon to discover part way into a meeting that a task one person took on earlier should be handled by a colleague. Passing the appropriate card provides the instant switch with minimal disruption.

Messages transmitted orally, said Pagonis in his Army days, "are too ephemeral to be effective. The 3 × 5, by contrast, doesn't go away. As it moves around, it physically nudges people into action. It's less of a solo manifesto and more of a group solution. . . . The 3 × 5 card system reinforces the idea of communality and teamwork."

SLIM-TRIMMERS FOR LEADERS

The following suggestions are for a meeting leader. If you already hold the position, they'll help you to facilitate "process," to avoid the almost exclusive attention to content that leads the angry and confused into the dead-end alleys of Fat City.

For some tips requiring written feedback, protect the identity of contributors, as suggested earlier, until rapport has been built. In short-term situations, however, allowing anonymity may be the only fast way to ensure that information needs and well-considered decisions aren't sabotaged or delayed. With each group and its objectives, weigh the trade-offs carefully.

Separate Tweedle Dum from Tweedle Dee. This technique works well at the first meeting of a committee in which many people already know each other. At each person's seat, put a small stack of white index cards on top of a copy of the agenda—printed on colored paper so it contrasts with the cards and is easily retrieved among handouts of white. On the top card, in large letters, print the person's name.

Upon entering the meeting room, most committee members will sit at their designated spots, and thus, without a big to-do, you can break up cliques, encourage new relationships, and affect the overall dynamics. At subsequent meetings of the group, repeat the procedure with a different seating arrangement. But be prepared for a few people to switch cards: Some Tweedle Dums (bless their knotted, little umbilical cords) can't part from their Tweedle Dees.

Set tone; get insights. At the beginning of a task force or similar group, invite participants to write answers to one of the following sets of questions. Have them give their responses aloud, then duplicate the cards for distribution as soon as possible. (Don't even bother to have them typed. Do be sure no one writes on both sides.) The cards will offer insights about each person's concerns, desires, and values—a time-saving key to effective debate and negotiation.

Note: If some members seem shy about responding out loud, bypass the step and route handouts of the reproduced cards, perhaps after taking a brief break to allow people to chat informally.

> "An Indian mongoose can reveal all with a single scent mark. The smell it leaves behind tells others who it is, how old it is, its place in the social hierarchy, its breeding condition, and even its mood."
>
> *Reader's Digest Exploring the Secrets of Nature*

Questions, Set A
- *What do I see as my key roles and responsibilities in this group?*
- *To be successful here, what do I need from my teammates?*
- *And what do I need to give my teammates?*
- *How do I see our team's work contributing to the organization's success?*

Questions, Set B
- *How will our customers benefit from this meeting?*
- *What specific things will occur in the meeting to ensure such an outcome?*
- *How do I plan to contribute to the meeting's success?*

Check for understandings. "I don't want to look stupid, so I'll just zip my lips." That attitude can prolong or ruin a meeting if people try to tiptoe around their gaps of understanding. Whenever you sense that might be happening—or to be sure it's not happening—invite committee members to complete one or more of the following statements on an index card before the group takes a break. If you wish, have the statements printed on an overhead transparency for repeated use:

- *I need definitions for _____.*
- *I'm still not quite sure I understand _____.*
- *It would help me to know more about _____.*
- *So far I feel comfortable with my understandings.*

The last entry ensures that everyone is seen writing and submitting a card.

Summarize periodically. "If I've followed the debate clearly, here are the four main points we've agreed to so far. Number one. . . ." When summaries are presented like this—and excellent leaders, I've observed, do it well and often—more meeting participants tend to jot down the points and remember them. That's particularly critical during teleconferences and videoconferences.

> **YANG: A leader should (1) recap from time to time as to where people are in the meeting and (2) give assignments from time to time. The leader needs to know—needs to be trained—that if someone doesn't recap every 20 minutes or 30 minutes, chances are things are going to be missed.**

Work with wishes. If a meeting hits a rough spot, and people are frustrated because they seem to be at cross purposes, stop the talk and ask each person to complete this statement about the meeting with no more than three responses:

I wish _____.

Then, if members do not object, have them read their copy as you note down and number the entries on an easel sheet, transparency, or copyboard—tick-marking repeated wishes. In one case, for example, the tick marks revealed what a majority of group members wanted to do next. Anger had been festering over a logjam. But thanks to the wish list and tick marks, participants acted upon the resulting signals and achieved a breakthrough that surprised even them.

Sometimes after a colleague has dared mention the unmentionable, others eagerly follow. Wish-givers, feeling really free to speak their minds, are quick to whack thickets with machetes.

Air arguments containing faulty assumptions, unsupported opinions, and misperceptions. When the timing is right and the need exists, say to a group, "Let's get out the clothesline," and "hang out" everyone's 3 × 5 cards. But work it figuratively, letting the gusts of wind (the healthy conflict of give-and-take) and the rays of sunshine (penetrating insights from the heat of debate) alter and freshen people's perspectives.

"Hanging out" the cards helps everyone examine the thoughts they're thinking—for it's thoughts, not people, that do battle. Moreover, the 3 × 5s serve to distance the process clinically, sufficiently. The "laundry's out there," flapping away for everyone to see and comment on in the collective search for new understandings.

Ideas needing exposure and scrutiny might come from responses to any of the following:

- *What assumptions—tested or untested—do you hear colleagues making?*
- *Which assumptions need to be suspended to ensure a free and open dialogue?*
- *Which assumptions or opinions, if any, are you still having a hard time accepting, and why?*
- *What perceptions do you hold that you're unsure about but would like to get some feedback on?*
- *Among colleagues' apparent misperceptions, which ones might negatively affect the outcome of this meeting?*
- *Do you detect any major gaps in the group's information base affecting this meeting? If so, what do they pertain to—stated in key phrases—and how might the gaps be filled?*

With a task force or similar group meeting over an extended period, a handout or an e-mail of the responses might be distributed before the next meeting to allow for reflection and for ready dialogue when the group reconvenes. Also consider using such questions in a survey if you suspect they deal with thoughts that could benefit from a good dose of sun and air.

NELSON: There's a difference in how an African-American male born in this country treats things versus how an African-American male like myself born in South America thinks about things. Yet when most people look at me, they only see me treating things the way a stereotypical African-American male does. In the African-American community, we are so diverse we can't get together to solve anything! It's true—it really is. Most others, though, see us as a homogenous group.

Assess the options; come to closure. To ferret out people's viewpoints about a particularly difficult or controversial topic, take an "instant survey" in which people write down their individual responses to a question, using a new card for each question posed. Here's one series that often puts a stop to seemingly endless debate:

- *What do you like about the option [proposal, position paper]?*
- *What concerns do you have about the option?*

Invite group members to respond in round-robin fashion to the first question as a volunteer numbers and records the key points on posted easel sheets, a large expanse of butcher paper, or a copyboard. Then proceed with the round(s) of replies to the second query.

After the first few responses, numbering allows participants to say things like "I agree with items 1, 2, and 5 . . . and would like to add two more." The process gets everyone to speak, the checkmarks next to repeated items help reveal a leaning or consensus, and the groundwork is set for the third and final question, if necessary:

- *Now that you've studied the easel sheets (notes on butcher paper or copyboard), what would it take for you to buy into the option?*

Questions, of course, may vary, and they don't have to be part of a series.

Effects of the exercise are fascinating. People often find they're more in agreement than not; the checkmarks are evidence. The introverts get a chance to verbalize, which may help reveal and solidify a consensus heretofore clouded by a vocal minority. The deliberation following a "new point" may nullify a concern, and the hang-backs who had relished playing their cards close to their chests are spurred into revealing their hands or giving the group a good peek. Once poker-faced, they now find it difficult not to say something positive and, after witnessing the openness of others, feel some obligation "to come clean." The debate, if it must continue, grows healthier.

Sometimes the concerns soon show that a particular option offers about as much opportunity as two bits at a Sotheby's auction. Thus, the group can make a swift cut and go on to another item. Chop! Chop!

FINCH: I like knowing from my staff if they're uneasy with some guidance I've given them. They need to tell me *early* so I can work with it. But if I've invested time, money, and effort in a certain course of action, and in the eleventh hour they come to me and say, "Oh, by the way, I can't support this decision [we're about to implement]," that's not playing fair.

Monitor tele-talkers. During a teleconference, trying to recall who said what to whom is as challenging as keeping abreast of positions taken by pandering politicians. Use cards to help you when there are no more than six or eight conferees. On each card, write the name of a conferee. In alphabetical order, lay the cards out or tape them in front of you. As someone makes a significant point, make note of it on the proper card, indicating in parentheses, when helpful, the name or initials of the person to whom the comment was directed:

LOREN

(GH) Radiation has to be sched.

For a teleconference with a large number of people, substitute for the cards a series of easel sheets or designated sections on a write-and-wipe wallboard or a wall of butcher paper. Have an assistant make entries so you need only glance at the board to facilitate the tele-talkers. For example: *Gwen, that brings us back to Loren's comment about scheduling the radiation. What are the prospects?*

METZGER: Teleconferences are not any different from on-site, face-to-face meetings; you still have to prepare, have an agenda, know what your goals are, and stick to them.

Follow up a teleconference or videoconference. To ensure everyone is on the same wavelength after holding a teleconference or videoconference with the sponsor of a task force, an executive council, or the like, ask meeting members to note on separate cards answers to these questions:

- What significant points did you hear? What do you think each means?
- What did you NOT hear? What might be the significance of each omission?

Round-robin the feedback, with each participant giving one response per round. List the replies on easel sheets, a wall of butcher paper, or a copyboard, and tick-mark recurring comments. Then share written feedback with the sponsor or council to correct any misunderstandings that might have occurred amid the seltzer bubbles of talk. For faxing copy from easel sheets, either have the copy typed or reproduce the sheets by taping them to a copyboard for printouts of reduced facsimiles.

For any task force dealing with an issue in which significant moneys are at stake, this kind of follow-up is an absolute must. Otherwise you run the risk of meetings becoming exercises in futility; participants would do just as well using Ouija boards or ESP.

Brainstorm. Involve everyone instantly. Have each member write as many ideas as possible on a single card or one idea per card, depending on the subsequent need to sort the ideas, swap the cards, reproduce them on a desktop copier in the room, or whatever. The technique produces more ideas faster—ideas that can also spawn other Ahas! when a compilation is viewed by the whole group.

It also provides the foundation for a round-robin feedback during which a reticent member may discover it's not so painful to say a phrase or two every

---

TO SEE OR NOT TO SEE

- Does the videoconference you're planning demand that any person, place, or thing be seen?

- Will the meeting involve more than just talking heads? If not, why is videoconferencing being used?

- Does something need to be demonstrated?

- Is it important that groups at different sites see the same thing at once?

- Will the videoconference save on time and travel?

- What will the video get-together accomplish that a teleconference with handouts (faxed, e-mailed, or delivered overnight) would not?

- If time is not critical, could a videotape of the information be sent to sites for viewing prior to a teleconference about the material?

---

now and then, thus possibly giving the person confidence to initiate ideas and express longer thoughts later on. In fact, to increase chances of that happening, you might have members exchange cards so they won't be contributing their own thoughts to the compilation.

Quick-rank items painlessly. Number the items in a list of choices shown on an easel sheet, overhead transparency, or copyboard. Ask participants to write each of their top three choices on separate index cards. Collect the cards, sort the "ballots" quickly, and announce the results, saving on the time-consuming process of ranking items orally in a round-robin fashion—a process that bores those who've cast their lots and thus sets them chattering.

Smoke out potential saboteurs. Just before a break, ask people to list questions about the issue being debated. Collect, reproduce, and distribute the questions when the timing seems best. This technique not only brings real concerns to the surface and helps prevent quick fixes, it also empowers the more introverted members and provides anonymity for those who think lobbing grenades will achieve their objective: blowing the issue to smithereens. Allowing the "lobbers" to vent like this is far safer than letting unaddressed concerns lead to extended, internecine warfare when the meeting adjourns.

Color-code the inquiries. Use colored index cards to collect questions about a schematic or mock-up, particularly during its developmental stage. As a speaker refers to a color-coded section, listeners write questions on cards of the same color. Questions might be recorded as they occur or during intervals signaled by the presenter. The objective is to gather as many queries as possible without fragmenting the big picture or the point the speaker is trying to convey.

As a variation uses different colored cards for categories of questions about a topic, e.g., technical questions (white), political (blue), logistical (yellow). After posting them, look for patterns, address each question, or both.

> During the Industrial Revolution, workers were displaced by machine-driven mills. The angry peasants threw their *sabots* (wooden shoes) into the works, thus giving rise to the word *sabotage*.

Take a group's pulse. From time to time, invite group members to rank on a scale of 1 to 5 how they think the meeting is going. Or ask them to draw a smiley, neutral, or frowning face to signal their mood; ask those who are disgruntled to explain why. Collect the cards just before a break and then, if necessary, work on adjusting the tenor of the meeting.

Similarly, have individuals rate the overall success of a meeting on a scale of 1 to 5, each giving a reason for the ranking. Have participants sign the cards, if they're willing to, so you can follow up with each person individually to benefit more from the feedback.

YANG: When you have 16 people in the room and half of them remain silent, then the quality of the meeting really degrades. On the other hand, if all of them speak it's going to be chaotic. Balance is necessary.

Hold up a cut-off warning signal. Cue Ivan the Interminable that he has five minutes left for his presentation.

You might also laminate the following signs made on colored paper:

PLEASE END YOUR "PRESO" AT 9:45	RECONVENE AT 2:10

Post the signs near the clock in the meeting room or alongside the one you hang up from your grab-and-go meeting kit. Just before a presentation or a break, tape a card inside the appropriate box while calling attention to the time designation you've marked on it.

Submit agenda items for the next meeting. Sometimes this is best done before adjourning the current meeting. Encourage committee members to follow the template shown on page 21, a squelcher of a fat-feeder.

5

the wars
of blubberco

Conquering meeting-breeding
e-mail and voice messages

Look what's happening at Blubberco.

With e-mail and other electronic messaging capabilities, more and more employees are spewing out, at lightning speed, tons of incoherent "stuff." Many missives, I suspect, might be considered first drafts at best. They're drafts in which the writer hasn't yet discovered exactly what she or he wants to say—documents filled with ambiguities, including unclear expectations. The messages may also consist of no more than two or three garbled lines in which clarity and conciseness have been sacrificed for speed and brevity, hardly General Pagonis's ideal.

In the form of voice messages, on the other hand, the "stuff" often results in circumlocutions gobbling up every allotted second—if there's a time restriction—and leaving listeners scratching their heads in wonder: What was *that* all about?

Further complicating the issue are automated

distribution lists, some of which rival the roster of runners for the Boston Marathon. Respondents on a long distribution list react in a variety of ways, especially when the message relates to a hot topic or comes from a VIP whose thoughts may be as prone to ambiguity as those of other mortals. In any event, here's what happens in too many cases:

- A few respondents ignore the e-mail or voice message. Click goes the delete key!

- Those familiar with the topic are most likely to jump in and respond to the best of their abilities, dashing off replies. Soon everyone in the subgroup, plus others they've sucked into their vortex, engages in electronic conversation, trying to unmuddy the ever-murkier mess. If they could be heard, they'd sound like magpies.

- People unfamiliar with the topic spawn their own missives and meetings to interpret the tarot cards. And who knows where, in the name of Beelzebub, those séances lead!

- Finally, among the top echelons of Blubberco, where paranoia runs rampant, those who think their territory has been invaded by what they read into the ambiguous message pull up their howitzers and blast off their rounds of e-mails, voice messages, and faxes, turning skirmishes into escalating electronic warfare. Big powwows are ultimately called to quell the fireworks.

In corporate America, such frenzy and fisticuffs, exacerbated by distribution lists, lie at the root of innumerable meetings. Start tracking them in your organization. They're among the quick-fix, whistle-blowing roundups called to solve crises.

One way to choke the meeting machines fueled by the fired-off "stuff" is to limit the lists or, like Charles B. Wang of Computer Associates International, pull the plug on the company's e-mail system for four hours a day (in the morning, from 10 till noon, and again in the afternoon, from 2 to 4). You can also encourage, or insist on messages—be they written or oral—that follow the Q&A format or that of the prompted All-Purpose Request whenever possible. Examples of both follow. Together, these techniques could level some healthy blows at the meeting-embattled Blubberco.

THE Q&A FORMAT

Realize that 80 percent of the time you interact with 20 percent of the same people. And when you interact with that 20 percent, 80 percent of the time you're seeking answers to questions. Hence, the Q&A format lends itself naturally to many "routine" e-mail messages and similar exchanges. For instance:

To:	Ailani Kimura@PA.MGR
From:	Phil Russell@G&A.P/P
Subject:	Staffing Cutbacks in Public Affairs
Date:	3/2/19__ 9:17 A.M.

Here are Qs you're likely to have—and my answers to them.

1. How do our figures compare to those projected by Phoenix?

   We're going to be hamstrung. M. Chu (Hdqtrs) wants seven. We need ten.

2. What are the figures based on?

   See fax sent 9:00 A.M. Kinslow has penciled in differences. We're also facing extra demands: (a) Annual Report—96 pp. and (b) more Bill Inserts (average of two more per mailing).

3. What effect will Chrona-Cron acquisition have?

   Hard to tell. Haven't received data yet. Am holding breath. Do same.

Also, some messages may seek answers to questions only:

Dear Leandro:

Techno-Logic ($750,000 revenue potential) needs answers to the following questions for a presentation to one of its clients on Tuesday. The Qs touch on your expertise. Your reply by this Friday will be fine.

1. What are . . . ?

2. How can . . . ?

3. When will . . .?

A question-and-answer exchange provides a kind of built-in quality-assurance test, for it encourages the originator of a message to stop for a few moments and wonder: *Will these queries get me exactly the information I'm looking for?* Seconds spent, meetings kaput.

SCHAFFER: When I get an e-mail message from a sales rep in country X describing a major deal, I may have six questions about it. I insert those questions, setting them off with single, horizontal carets. The sales rep marks replies with double vertical carets. That way, the original message is kept intact. Besides, it's very easy to rub someone the wrong way with e-mail. (There's no body language and that kind of thing.) Even if you're sure the other person has screwed up, you must be very polite and respectful. Life is tense enough.

THE ALL-PURPOSE REQUEST

In managing conversations and commitments, you spend much of your time making requests (or recommendations) and responding to them. You can save gobs of time and energy by communicating with this series of prompts for the body text:

- REQUEST OR RECOMMENDATION
- BENEFIT(S)
- BACKGROUND
- ACTION
- TIME ON TASK
- RESULTS OF DELAY
- DEADLINE

The prompts don't always have to be used in that sequence, though it's the most common. Prompts can be rearranged, added, or deleted, depending on the "story" you want to tell.

The formula also rescues poor to average writers, since the prompts scrap the need for transitions, while the sequence helps ensure a coherent message. In short, the format eliminates or minimizes not only the meetings that muddy messages spawn but also the get-togethers people call because they're reluctant to write in the first place—a source of meeting overload that seems to be spreading faster than a February flu.

The outline for the generic request offers many advantages:

- It gets to the bottom line immediately.

- It forces the writer to consider the benefit (the *why* of the *what*). If the benefit isn't clear to the writer or appears nonexistent or insignificant, then the writer is not likely to send the message. What a boon!

- Background doesn't clog up the beginning of a message as it usually does when a writer feels the need to begin with the genealogy of Methusalah.

- If the action requires more than one step, numbering the steps and beginning them with verbs forces the writer to consider these questions: *Have I included all the necessary steps? Are the steps precise? Does the reader have the authority and/or resources to take the steps? Will completing the steps fulfill the request or support the recommendation?*

- Suggesting time on task helps connote the scope and level of detail expected in completing the steps. This information is particularly important when the request goes from a boss (the parent figure) to a direct report (the child who may tries to engender the parent's embracing glow by doing more than asked).

- Sometimes telling the reader what will happen if she or he doesn't move on the request spurs the person into action. In a highly political environment, this prompt and its message works wonders.

- Giving reasons for a specific deadline prevents many an ASAP!

Think: If most missives were required to be "benefit-driven"—especially with the customer in mind—many e-mails, voice messages, and attendant meetings would go the way of the wind. In the messages that survived, clear benefit statements would help employees better determine their priorities.

In the thousands of documents I see from year to year, benefits are either not clearly cited or not cited at all. (Voice messages suffer the same drawback.) Besides the aura of an originator's signature (in a hierarchical setting) or an obviously critical topic, there's nothing by which to judge the relative importance of the pieces. So employees work far into the nights and weekends to catch up on their correspondence, to assure themselves that, if there is something important on the screen or in the stack of papers, it won't, by default, go unattended. What they don't realize is that they're often shackled with hastily related, ambiguous missives, where respect for the word could replace stress with rest and a heaping-up of the coffers.

How It Works

The following sample shows the REQUEST and BENEFIT combined. Notice, too, the ACTION plan; numbering the steps in a checklist setup helps ensure a reader's accuracy and the likelihood of complete implementation. Finally, in the copy for DEADLINE, the writer suggests a certain amount of TIME ON TASK. RESULTS OF DELAY could have been prompted, but in this case a gentler warning wraps up the action steps.

> Dear Sandy:
>
> REQUEST/BENEFIT: By extending our newspaper coverage into Fulsom and Rodgers counties, we might be able to attract the 25- to 35-year-old customers moving into those areas.
>
> BACKGROUND: During the past five years, new housing in the counties has risen a combined 14 percent. *Realtors' Newsline* reported in May that more than 150 houses turned over, and the majority of new buyers were young families. The Fulsom Unified School District is also talking about building two new elementary schools.
>
> ACTION: Let's plan to run a coupon offer in next Tuesday's *Clarion* to see what kind of response we get. To that end, please:
>
> __1. Adapt the ad we used in the Laramie campaign last March.
>
> __2. Take out a quarter page in the *Clarion's* "Marketplace."
>
> __3. Alert Angela at the copy desk.
>
> Tuesday's edition includes the newcomer's insert, which always gets a big readership. Missing it would be a shame.
>
> DEADLINE: A half hour on your end, Sandy, should do things up fine, since the Laramie ad needs little tweaking. Besides, you'll

need to fax your copy to Angela for final approval no later than 11 on Friday morning. Thanks for handling.

An ACTION section may also indicate concurrent steps:

Would you be sure to:

__1. E-mail Roger in Bangkok

__2. Set up a teleconference for next Monday at 3 P.M. Denver time

Meanwhile, I will:

__1. Route the advance reading materials

__2. Prepare the tentative agenda for the conference

Or steps that are consecutive:

Please have your doctor route us a copy of the bill for your hospital visit. Upon receipt, we will:

__1. Verify that coverage is allowed under Plan B

__2. Update you on your options if coverage is not allowed

OR send a check for 90 percent of the bill

To see how this fat-curbing formula helps meetings directly, see pages 51 and 52.

VOICE MESSAGES

With voice mail, the approaches above—modified as needed—can turn messages of mincemeat into clear, concise English.

LEAVING A VOICE MESSAGE THAT'S
EASY TO FOLLOW

1. Limit your message to an oral version of the 3 × 5.

2. Remember: Your listener can't "pre-hear" what you're going to say, so before dialing, jot down points you want to make, keeping in mind steps 3 to 6.

3. Get to the bottom line by the second sentence.

4. Ask your key questions or adapt the All-Purpose Request.

5. Give verbal signposts (e.g., "First," "Second") to your questions or action steps.

6. Cite your deadline and preferred medium of response.

SAMPLE: *Jean, this is Rod Wilson, extension 4667. I have three questions about the Incident Report from yesterday. Number one[PAUSE]: When was the Landon call received? Number two [PAUSE]: Did anyone follow up with the systems administrator? Number three [PAUSE]: Who supervises the third shift? Call or fax me before you leave today. Our customer is claiming a discrepancy. Again, my phone is 4667 [PAUSE]. My fax is 3276. Thanks.*

LETTING YOUR VOICE GREETING WORK FOR YOU

1. Change your greeting daily, so a caller trying to reach you for a meeting isn't left wondering if you're on a freighter to Pango Pango.

   SAMPLE: *Hello, this is Eddie Whitaker. Today is May 12, and I'll be in my office all day except for a videoconference between 9 and 10:15. If your message demands an immediate reply, please call Casey Abrams at 444-2037.*

2. Consider a greeting that takes advantage of the 80/20 rule. Train your most frequent callers to be ready with specific, time-saving queries.

   SAMPLE: *Hello, this is Janisa Dorran. Today is October 5. If you have specific questions, please leave them at the sound of the beep, and I'll get back with answers as soon as I can. But if you need something else, please explain briefly.*

6 beware the frost heaves— join AA

Fostering and implementing significant changes that facilitate meeting management

Around my way, some of the finest wholesale pruning is done in the fall, by nor'easters thundering up the New England coast. Rain sheets and gales of wind serve notice even to the stalwart maples, whose tough old trunks drip the sap of spring.

But between December and the final weeks of March, Mother Nature alters our land slowly, imperceptibly, inexorably. With the frost heaves of winter, she topples stones from the walls rimming meadows. She hummocks winding country roads. She tilts the mailboxes and, with the deepest of sighs, buckles the Shaker-gray sheds of yesteryear.

Changes like those—some obvious and instant, some subtle and slow—affect meeting management as well.

In chapters 2 to 4, you read primarily about ideas you can act on individually, immediately. No guts required. No ladders of approval. But this chapter looks at streamliners that can have significant, widespread effects, and the related changes often demand new behaviors of others. These changes may also disrupt deeply rooted routines that are outrageously profligate in terms of time and money. Altering these routines to affect the value and volume of meetings demands tact, patience, and tenacity. For the most sweeping and enduring changes come less from the prunings of an occasional nor'easter and more from the topplings and tiltings of unremitting frost heaves.

So take a deep sigh. Set your sights. Be selective. And begin.

Join AA. To exert pressure for quality-based, well-run meetings in your organization, become an Alignment Advocate. Each member of AA believes that by inspiring and leading people toward a vision shared, understood, and subscribed to, wasted motion in attaining the vision becomes—idealistically speaking—nil. The group's motto is *Why we are here matters; where we are going matters more.*

Absence of alignment, however, causes chaos in objective-setting to one degree or another, creating an uncertain, ever-shifting terrain on which thrive many meeting troublemakers. It's an endless feeding ground for negativists, vacillators, and whiners, as well as intimidators, subversives, and their counterproductive kin, because all of them can consciously or unconsciously satisfy the needs basic to their behavior.

But with alignment encouraging more and more people to follow their individual and collective paths to a shared, clearer vision, the negative behaviors that eat into meeting time and beget other meetings become more transparent and risky. The troublemakers begin to realize: I'd better get with the program—or I'll be steamrolled.

LA ROSA: You can't expect the people working for you to intuit what's going on and what the goals are—for they are shifting goals often. You have to struggle to get the clarity of vision in the first place.

FINCH: A corporation needs a vision and measurable goals and objectives. Within that context, if you have a little wiggle room, that's okay, but if you *lack* the vision, *lack* the direction, then ad hoc items tend to control the company; they take over the day.

Unfortunately, many organizations haven't even thought about a shared vision, and in companies where I have observed framed vision statements on the walls, most attempts at alignment get either bottlenecked or aborted, at least tacitly. Here's why, I believe: With eye on the coin, not the word, the latter, which is fundamental to inspiration and direction-setting, is virtually ignored. For it is words—most often words exchanged in the context of meetings, including hallway bump-ins—that leaders use to build and cement relationships as they manage conversations and commitments. And the better these leaders' language skills complement their technical expertise, the more likely it is that alignment will become a dynamic that energizes and streamlines meetings.

It's a snap to recognize the leaders and participants who have taken the AA 12-Step Pledge on pages 56–57:

Play the organ. Whether it's slick or quick-n-dirty, a newsletter, magazine, or other company house organ provides an excellent instrument for keeping effective meeting management on the collective conscience of employees. Encourage the editor to start a feature, to write success stories, to interview the CEO as a champion of the cause. As the running of good meetings becomes a publicly valued and acclaimed skill, you'll see diets of fat-chat give way to couscous and alfalfa sprouts.

KNOSKA: My staff and I don't get together often, but when we do, I like to lead the meeting with these three questions: (1) What are we doing well? (2) What aren't we doing so well? and (3) What aren't we doing at all and should be?

"Don't generate, locate." That was the advice a VP gave his colleagues. Instead of forming another task force, he said, find out if similar work has already been done and documented or if it's occurring in another arena. He wanted to stop the right hand from not knowing what the left was doing—until it was too late.

To handle that kind of challenge and reduce meeting overlap, encourage management to consider the following:

- Require the chair of a new committee to complete the form below and post it on a special corridor bulletin board or adapt it to an electronic bulletin board or notebook.

THE AA 12-STEP PLEDGE

1. I will do all in my power to ensure that my organization's statement of vision is simple, direct, and clear to all with whom I work, including customers, associates, and suppliers.

2. I, like many an inspiring and results-oriented leader, will seek a vivid metaphor that enables all in my work community—or at least in my particular sphere—to picture a common image around which individuals and groups can map and execute their way toward the shared vision.

3. I will view myself, no matter what my official job title, as a manager of conversations and commitments in webs of relationships—a perspective that will help alignment by sensitizing me to the significance of words that are well chosen, well timed, and well placed.

4. I, as a leader, will write my own speeches and other major "public messages," edited, perhaps, by associates, but uncontaminated by sycophants. It is absolutely and unquestionably essential that I be heard in *my* voice, sharing anecdotes based on *my* own observations and using words that consistently reveal *my* credibility and *my* constancy about the shared vision.

5. I will do more than merely talk about the need to break boundaries. I will ensure that everyone, including me, has the tools and training in collaboration, negotiation, and meeting management to speed and ease the toppling of barriers.

6. I will take advantage of emerging technologies to see that fresh, illustrative, and inspirational success stories about employees helping to fulfill the vision are spread throughout the organization *daily*, so the community's constancy about the vision, which may at first seem abstract and remote to some—especially when it is alluded to only in a quarterly publication of dead news—eventually encompasses an ever-widening circle of engagement.

THE AA 12-STEP PLEDGE
(continued)

7. I will neither clutter the roads of alignment nor fog up the vision with tangential programs and campaigns that change with the seasons.

8. I will ensure that associates and I share not only a clear understanding and an unwavering belief in our objectives but a desire and commitment to see that those objectives become equally understood and subscribed to in our wider community, where fulfilling organizational objectives depends on a multitude of specific, discrete actions meaningful to the individual performers.

9. As a delegator, I will take the time to explain a request; as a delegatee, I will seek explanation and clarification because I realize, in most cases, people will perform the *what* more efficiently, effectively, and even creatively when they understand and support the *why*, especially when the *what* of a subtle or sudden shift in direction is related to the *why* of a changing need in the marketplace.

10. I will become a paragon of a meeting leader, viewing gatherings of all sorts and sizes as the primary vehicles through which members of the work community manage most of the conversations and commitments that, when understood precisely and acted upon decisively, drive us toward realization of the vision.

11. I will not view empowerment as a dubbing ceremony but rather the motivation that comes to me by clearly understanding a vision I can appreciate, share, and respect; acting on that understanding in the best way I can; and gaining a greater sense of self-worth from having done so with success and satisfaction.

12. I will keep asking myself: *No matter how simple and obvious this pledge may seem, am I truly fulfilling it? Perhaps most importantly, am I sticking to it with steadfast determination?*

- Encourage editors of the company house organ to establish a column on task-force updates. (Snails, beware!)

- Establish a library for documents produced by committees and task forces.

By making the number of special committees tangible, people begin to see where meeting overload is a major problem. They think twice about forming other groups. They find ways to combine efforts. They narrow issues—especially when they have to write abstracts—and even use Parkinson's Law to the advantage of shorter deadlines. But when information exchange about new committees and their objectives is oral, casual, and barely existent, there's little but occupied meeting rooms to cause anyone to shout "Fat alert! Fat alert!"

COMMITTEE ABSTRACT

Name of Committee: _____

Chairperson: _____

Telephone: _____ Fax: _____

E-mail: _____

Abstract: _____

_____

_____

Key Words—in Alphabetical Order—of Topics to be Covered:

_____

_____

Starting Date: _____ Ending Date: _____

Kennel the dogs! Corral those ponies! As the story goes, the Duchess of Birmingham presented Queen Henrietta Maria a king-size pie. Out of it popped Jeffrey Hudson, a 19" dwarf who won the queen's heart and a job as Her Majesty's court jester.

Have times changed? Not much if you consider those dog-and-pony shows for the boss and royal biggies. No jesters, perhaps, but a lot of fools cavorting around, making slides, testing mikes, polishing lecterns, producing videos, ensuring dissolves, adjusting the kliegs, and rehearsing, rehearsing, rehearsing. What a gigantic circus and a carryover from medieval fetes, the Lipizzaner drill, the Westminster Dog Show! And at the center of this drama lies tension: Who will be harlequin or win Best in Class?

Now I'll admit there may be times for such spectacles, such as major conventions (and at that I have to do mental gymnastics to justify the expense), but the hoopla and the costs and the lost opportunities and the absences from real work are certainly unwarranted for a quarterly or annual review with the CEO or lower-ranking regents. In fact, such razzle-dazzle should be banished from the royal household.

WANG: Communicate! Don't just show up with overheads to give a big two-hour production for the CEO. If that happens to me, I say, "I don't have time for those slides. You may have people who love them, but I don't. Let's assume you've got the best of whatever and take it from there. Get away from your sales pitch. Let's interact."

Instead of smoke and mirrors, people might achieve more with a few prepared overhead transparencies complemented by easel-sheet jottings, other transparencies made on the spot, or their electronic equivalents.

Instead of disengaged voices in a darkened room, let people see each other's faces, probe each other's thoughts, focus on the future, and bask less in the past. In the process, coins will be saved in the royal treasury (away with rehearsals, my lord!), ideas will grow more fecund, and who knows how much richer will become the company pie.

Save on Excedrin. Make the improvement of meetings an item for deliberation at your next get-together, perhaps prompted by a brief video or an excerpt from a publication. Frame the matter. Don't try to effect too many changes at once.

Next Wednesday let's take 20 minutes or so to look at the way our meetings have been going. This article got me thinking, as I'm sure it will you. It could save on Excedrin and who knows what else! Please read it and be ready to share your thoughts during a round-robin of feedback. (*Note:* The last sentence indicates to slough-offs that they'll be expected to respond publicly, which might prod them into actually reading the item.)

DELMONT: For every quarterly sales meeting, we have a post mortem. All attendees critique the meeting. We [as conveners] critique ourselves because we're not happy with our meetings yet. We still don't think we're there. We still have a lot of things to improve on.

Poll the Dash-and-Dos. At the end of a meeting, consider distributing a simple evaluation form similar to the one that follows. It takes less than a minute to complete and thus accommodates the sprinters.

√	Please rate this meeting on a scale of 10 (highest) to 1	☺ 10	9	8	7	☺ 6	5	4	3	2	☹ 1
A	This meeting was worthwhile.										
B	We kept focused.										
C	Participation was high.										
D	We got things done.										
To improve our next meeting, I suggest we:											

Hold them accountable. Perhaps your organization has, or is considering, a 360-degree evaluation system, one in which everyone who works with a person—boss, peers, and direct reports—contributes to that person's appraisal. If that's the case where you are, build into the stakeholders' survey a series of very specific, observable items about meeting management, such as: (1) works by agenda and action-plan take-aways, (2) focuses mainly on customer benefits, and (3) uses process-oriented techniques to help groups gain new insights.

Say "Hogwash!" to Mondays. Besides Thanksgiving dinner with an extended family, nothing murmurs with more undercurrents than one of those status-report meetings, usually held on Monday mornings, at which people sit in the same chairs and play the same familial, stereotypical roles: good daughter, go-getter son, competitive cousin, demanding parent, fidgety aunt, irascible uncle.

Unless it's a quick stand-up, catch-up meeting—or a teleconference parallel—most of these powwows need to be killed, at least in their traditional form: as weekly round-robin rituals of sibling rivalry. Most of the time, a Parent Figure simply holds a series of one-on-one conversations, while other "family" members, pretending to await their turns on Pappy's lap, are either tuning out the whole event or mentally rehearsing their little pieces of fiction.

PEEPLES: I know of a staff meeting that goes from 2:00 to 7:00 each week. Problem: no agenda. It's just a free-for-all, and they wonder, "How did we end up in Peoria?"

HOWELL: If you can find interlocking objectives that force people to work together—from sales to service to delivery, for example—then you, as a manager, don't have to have those meetings where everybody goes around to show and tell.

Today, with computers and fax machines as well as software packages that provide or create fill-in-the-blank templates, most oral status reporting should be replaced by clear, accurately written information available when needed—not minutes or days later, when it's too late, too stale.

"But oh," say some, "the Monday meeting is the one time we can get together to do team building, to hear about what others are up to." Hogwash! The form, as it's usually practiced, doesn't allow for that. Even a modicum of team building, if it occurs then, is strictly happenstance. Observe how participants separate into islands and little, impenetrable ghettos.

If team building is the objective, then islands must merge, ghettos must tumble. And if the objective is to learn what others are *really* doing, then penguins had better beckon the robins. Awaiting the objectives are other vehicles—more effective, less fattening, and a lot more fun. Just tap your imagination.

IF YOU INSIST ON A WEEKLY POWWOW . . .

- Help a meeting participant strategize on a difficult account.

- Analyze the culture of a new organization you're dealing with.

- Distribute an article about a team toppling silos. Explore parallels.

- Round-robin: *Here's an idea I heard about. . . . How might we adapt?*

- Assess: *What expectations do our clients buy? What are the elements of each expectation? What might clients expect next?*

- Conduct a demo of a communication tool people need to know better.

- Explore: *What does this news clipping mean for us?*

- Invite a speaker from a different field, seeking ideas to build on.

- Examine a process in terms of "commitment steps" and the need for clear, precise language at each step.

- Round-robin: *Here's my blooper and what I learned from it.*

- Ask: *Where have you experienced excellent service lately, what steps constituted the service, and how might they be adapted here?*

Conduct an autopsy. Next time there's a crisis, examine what you think launched it. Then probe the next crisis. And the next. Look for patterns. In most every case, the cause will not be a mechanical breakdown but a communication snafu. Here, for example, are three of the common fat adders and how they can be prevented:

PROBLEM: The boss barks something in a shorthand: "Look into it right away." Or a document is routed with an elliptical or cryptic cover note, such as:

- FYA (for your action)
- What's your input?
- Is there something here?

- Any thoughts?
- Any suggestions?
- Read and get back to me.

SOLUTION: If you're the boss, particularly in a hierarchical organization, become aware of the "oral shorthand" you use (ask a secretary to tell you); your position often imbues a comment with more layers of meaning than you may realize. Better yet, make yourself an electronic template or preprinted routing note of your frequently made requests. Then all you have to do is check off which clearly worded instruction you'd like a delegatee to act on. For example:

[ ] *See underscores. Are they points we need to monitor? Why or why not?*

If you're the delegatee in one of these situations, tell the delegator, "I want to make sure we're in tune. Here's what I believe you're expecting me to do . . . ." Even though it may take courage to pause for clarification, it's far less painful than withstanding a tirade triggered by your failure to understand.

PROBLEM: A senior official's casual remark is interpreted as an edict by a sycophant. The direct report, wanting to brown-nose the boss, churns up tornadoes of meetings. *Note:* One customer's request to a sales representative can have similar effects.

SOLUTION: Fire off questions and concerns: "What exactly did she say? I want to make sure you don't end up with mud in your face." Or "Could you tell me the benefits he's driving at? It would help me figure out how to get you exactly what you need as fast as I can." Be sure the delegator knows you have his or her best interests in mind. *You-you-you-er* to death. After a few questions, watch the edict melt into an "if-you-can-get-to-it." Phew! Dump, dump!

PROBLEM: A decision is made without properly identifying it and/or determining what criteria the optimal solution should meet.

SOLUTION: In problem-solving, become the watchdog on those two matters only. Colleagues will automatically take care of other steps, such as brainstorming, citing examples, debating the pros and cons.

Be sure, not sorry. "Jump!" the client shouts. "How high?" the supplier asks. This all too typical, Pavlovian response sets off a chain reaction, sometimes of global proportions—literally, electronically. Whatever the customer wants, the rep has been told implicitly if not explicitly, "Get it done!" Though that may be the competitive charge, it seldom justifies the following:

- failure to probe the customer about the immediate request

- failure to ask the customer to cite examples of the problem—anecdotes that might reveal the need for a completely different solution, one that may already be on the shelf

- failure to educate the customer from the beginning about the processes attendant to the project

- failure to find out about the customer's customer

- failure, *throughout* the sales cycle, to interrogate the customer constantly about specific wants and needs so the process of discovery is less prone to the inevitable spurs and spurts

- failure to bring the home-based support staff into the sales loop soon enough . . . and the list goes on.

The cycle, which the customer's customer has probably instigated, reminds me of a sign posted in many art and production departments: Your lack of planning doesn't constitute my emergency.

The failures listed often spring from a dearth of serious, well-planned meetings in which understandings should be reached and recorded. Instead, firefighting rules the day and inflames the ulcers.

SCHAFFER: Trips overseas, in my book, should not be reserved for VPs, directors, and product-line managers. Order-operations people and order-entry people should meet their customers face to face. In fact, just two hours ago I heard that our Euro-wide order-entry people are attending such a meeting week after next. That's the kind of investment we believe in. It's not cheap traveling to Europe, but it pays off in spades.

KNOSKA: I tell everybody, You have the customer buying the product, plus all the people supporting the deal. My grandfather, for instance, owned a grocery store during the Depression. Whenever my father, a kid then, walked through the store, he'd see tons of salt. One day he said, "Gee, we must sell a lot of salt." "No," said my grandfather, "*the guy who sells us a lot of salt* sells a lot of salt." That supplier, you see, was selling the end customer as well as a person in the support group.

Exclaim, "Surely templates are a must!" Legions of meetings are called to gather information that could easily be supplied by asking the sources of the data to complete templates. Besides the usual statistical forms, the following fill-in-the-blanks and check-offs provide a range of savings beyond their immediate benefits:

1. Questions to be answered yes, no, or maybe about a litany of categorized requirements or specifications

2. Questions numerically keyed to responses (e.g., *Always, Sometimes, Never*) that:
   - help customers distinguish needs from wants and wishes
   - reveal meaningful expectations rather than premature specifications

3. Templates on how to write a:
   - quick turnaround business case or a response to an RFP
   - charge or mandate for a task force or subcommittee proposal, including verb-driven recommendations as well as a cover letter or executive summary highlighting chief differentiators

4. Checklists that:
   - help employees give each other snapshots of job-related information that can quickly determine if and when a person needs to be included in the loop on a topic
   - make respondents distinguish features from benefits and applications

Get the idea? There are numerous possibilities.

Any template above, if not used, could spawn a Medusa of meetings in which the one-time, careful wording of a form to cull precise, complete information would be replaced by endless rounds of huh-n-whadjasay talk.

Try lunch á la Microsoft. Instead of lunching with the same ol' gang, pick up the phone and invite someone to lunch from another department.

Managers spend 60 percent of their time within their own department boundaries, according to Dr. Raymond Panko, professor of decision sciences at the University of Hawaii. "People don't like distance," Panko says. "Beyond 75 feet, people talk very little . . . [which is] frightening [because] talking locally within one's department tends to fragment the organization."

At Microsoft, an apparent exception to Panko's findings, Excel developers hold "brown-bag" lunches "where people talk about different areas of code to help new people learn the product and to familiarize experienced people with changes or areas they did not know about yet." Similarly, program managers hold "blue tray" lunches that are videotaped for circulation.

You, too, can substitute something for gossip over goulash. Learn about what's happening "out there" and who's making it happen, so you can have up-to-date information to share in meetings. You'll add luster to your authority, become savvy about the lingo and ways of other cultures in the organization, help colleagues speed their learning curves, and, at times, be able to keep meetings from folding for lack of information—a major cause of grousing and regrouping.

Be subversive. With three or four friends, publish a one-page, irregular, underground flyer on meetings. Keep the group a deep, dark secret, but give yourselves a name: Meeting Choppers, Wannabe Productive, Inc., or maybe M&M (meetings and memos) Limited.

Post the bulletin—clandestinely, of course—where knots of people gather. Get them looking forward to the releases, conjecturing about their authorship, debating your points and—miracle of miracles!—actually acting on them.

> "One of the things my father didn't teach me was how to quit."
>
> *Herman Cain, President*
> *Godfather's Pizza, Inc.*

Who knows, you might catch the attention of the official company newspaper and reach management's movers and shakers in ways you couldn't otherwise. At the same time, you'll uphold a great American tradition harking back to the pamphlet-producing revolutionaries of the 1700s. They certainly knew about nor'easters and the frost heaves of winter.

part II

CULINARY TEAMWORK

"No restaurant can run successfully without teamwork. Each member of the team has a role to play, and must play it well, or there is no ultimate victory. As a leader. . . . I encourage spontaneity and welcome the contributions of each member of the team. Together we can reach even higher."

Charlie Trotter
Master Chef

7

"and the Oscar goes to . . ."

Mastering the roles of a leader

Effective meeting leaders deserve Oscars. They not only have to employ a number of techniques, but they also must play a variety of roles. Mastery of the craft comes from practice, practice, practice, meeting after meeting.

That's how I learned—and am *still* learning. Every meeting presents another opportunity to refine a technique, to correct a past mistake, to try something new, to risk, to stretch, to grow. That's the challenge as well as the fun. But because effective meeting leadership is so demanding, some people prefer to absolve themselves of any such responsibility: They're the abdicators, the gutless wonders. Others prefer to play a single role only, the easiest of all: dictator.

That role requires little more than scare tactics and the growls of a Doberman. Not even a grade-school diploma is needed for it—just heavy amounts of amorality and perhaps some steel-lined, ulcer-proof intestines. Much more difficult is playing a range of roles, where the risks for a leader may at first seem daunting but ultimately prove rewarding.

Thus, the choices are few. You can be an abdicator or a dictator, or you can begin to master the repertoire that follows and shape the parts to your unique personality and talents. For out of the fires of trial and error—of playing the roles and growing more and more comfortable with them—are forged the real strengths of meeting leadership, at the core of which must be the ability to remain true to yourself and your beliefs.

Host

Making participants feel comfortable with the setting and each other calls for the talents and concerns of an amiable dinner host. But when participants are treated like total strangers, the leader acts like a condescending butler, and what's being offered on the agenda/menu is anyone's guess—a combination of events I see quite often—then the get-together is likely to turn into either of two things: funeral or food fight.

Researcher

Treat each meeting as a laboratory experiment, even trying some of the Instant Shrinkers without further delay. Observe what works and doesn't work. Particularly after a meeting is over, replay it in your mind. Ask yourself:

- Did the meeting work? Why or why not?
- Was the customer on the minds of the participants? If so, how was that evident? If not, why not?
- Who or what surprised me in the meeting, and why?
- What failed, and why? What can I learn from that failure?
- Was the conflict about [topic] healthy or not? On what observable criteria do I base my judgment?
- How did people challenge and handle assumptions?

Facilitator

As a constant learner and observer, be alert to certain procedures that help individuals as well as the group. (For an excellent matrix of facilitation skills, see "The Secrets of Team Facilitation" by Greg Burns, *Training and Development*, June 1995, page 49.) You may happen upon certain procedures serendipitously, plow through some painfully, or both. But if you don't record the steps of a process that worked, you'll forget it and end up repeatedly furrowing hard, new soil. Conversely, you may realize that certain failures stemmed from letting a committee lurch about without suggested processes—*a major cause of fat-jammed meetings*—and now you have insights into what might work the next time.

That's how I compiled my Facilitator's Handbook, which includes not only master copies of handouts that help participants with expectations and attitudes but also a number of transparencies outlining steps in brainstorming, requirement gathering, problemsolving, decision making, ranking of items, and so on. (Chapter 11 includes samples.) For each process I have a dozen or so different approaches; the 80/20 rule accounts for the two or three used most often. But because work groups, organizational subcultures, and dynamics differ, I also suggest alternatives. Thus, until a group becomes familiar with a certain needed process, begins to favor one over another, or determines a variation of its own, I can select which transparency to project and keep the meeting on track by suggesting why the group is most likely to benefit from following those particular steps at that particular time.

What a lard-lopping life-saver the handbook has become. Yours will, too.

Futurist

Keep the group's collective eye on the future. By networking informally, reading and reflecting, and tapping into whatever research mechanisms your organization may have or have access to, become aware of trends and patterns that could affect your business, your customers, and others involved in that relationship. From time to time, present agendas that focus solely on the future. And in your day-to-day meetings and conversations, raise questions that help ingrain such an orientation in the culture. For example:

- *Six months from now, what will this decision mean for our customers?*
- *If we were to go with that alternative, how might the company look in 18 months? Is that projected image worth the risk? Why or why not? If there is a major risk, what might be done to minimize it?*
- *Who are our future competitors likely to be? Which ones are not even on the radar screen yet? Should we worry about them now? Why or why not?*

By being future-directed in meetings, you can come at the issues of alignment from a slightly different angle, helping team members see, for example, the *whys* of a significant *what* and the links to the vision. At the same time, the focus can renew a group's energy by revealing opportunities or creating a healthy sense of anxiety that catapults team members from their inertia. In short, putting a face on the future gives those who peer into it not only a better sense of proportion about issues and priorities but also a sense of urgency that translates into regaining and maintaining momentum.

Manager of Expectations

Rather than simply saying to yourself "I've *got* to get this done," stop—even for just a few moments—and think "Who's expecting *what* (in the way of output) and *why* (for what benefits) when I start the meeting I'm about to call?" Depending on the situation, the expectations vary, from the boss and attendees, to associates, suppliers, customers, and you.

LA ROSA: If I don't hear from my direct reports, I assume they're doing what they're supposed to be doing and not having a problem. But if they are having a problem, I fully expect them to share it with me. Working like this starts with the hiring process. You've got to hire people who understand the method.

The Boss

Too often his or her expectations are tacit. People operate based on conjectures about what the boss wants, and that's when they get into trouble. A clear sense of the vision, plus alignment, can guide many a meeting in terms of what the boss would expect in general; but when it comes to major get-togethers for specific, significant output, such as a task force, it's critical that you and your boss, or whoever is the sponsoring agent, agree on the group's written charter, or mandate. No seltzer bubbles of talk, please.

1. In the charter, include at least the following:
   - Purpose: Why is the group being assembled, and what events—particularly as they relate to the vision—have brought about this need?
   - Scope: What is the committee to do?
   - Limitations: What is *not* to be included in the scope of the group's work?
   - Deliverable(s): What is the output to be, and what forms should it take?
   - Milestones: What are the checkpoint dates?
   - Deadline: When is the group to complete its task and disband?

2. Limit the charter to one page or less.

3. Draft it yourself; then collaborate with the boss in editing and clarifying. Otherwise you're likely to meet resistance: "I don't have time for that. Just go ahead and get it done."

4. Present the charter at the first meeting of the task force, encouraging members to question and clarify, preferably with the boss available in person or on a speakerphone to join in the deliberation. (After all, she or he is to be held accountable as well.) If appropriate, agree on changes in the wording.

Note: If the boss cannot take part in the kick-off and questions do arise about the language of the charter, be sure to share immediately—by e-mail, fax, or other written form—what phrasing(s) were unclear to the group and why. In short, work back and forth—two times or more if necessary, even while proceeding with the first day's agenda—to ensure that everyone, including the boss, is singing from the same hymnal. It may take time (in one group it took two days because the members themselves had to generate a charge for a task calling for a multimillion-dollar decision), but recall what Plato wisely observed: "The beginning is the most important part of the work."

PHILLIPS: In preparing for a meeting, it helps to gain strong management sponsorship and to produce a first draft of every written deliverable. A good policy is never to come to the table with a blank sheet of paper. With that kind of preparation, plus a charter and agenda, people are amazed at how a team can accomplish so much quality work in so little time.

The Attendees

They decide, no matter your degrees or title, what kind of a leader you'll be—and whether you're a success or failure, based on how well you measure up to their expectations. Each participant completes a mental checklist like the one below. And your job as a meeting leader is to use your antennae and tap the advice and techniques herein so you can discern and exceed the expectations. How do you think you'd do?

[ ] Knows who he or she is and, despite his or her unique personality and style, holds to an unswerving set of beliefs and values.

[ ] Seeks to understand who each of us is, seeing us not as automatons to help him or her achieve selfish goals but as unique human beings sharing journeys on planet Earth.

[ ] Recognizes the preciousness of our time, cherishes it, and protects it—a true believer in the ''Twinge Test'' (see page 17).

[ ] Makes no effort to manipulate us for a predetermined outcome—never even considers the option—because we can smell a rat faster than a barnyard cat.

[ ] Shows patience with people and the collaborative process, for discovering anything worthwhile almost never happens cleanly, directly, or immediately.

[ ] Frees and inspires us by trusting us, a hallmark of the servant-leader.

[ ] Celebrates the individuality of each of us while wedding our knowledge and talents for the good of all.

[ ] Has a clear sense of where she or he is leading us and why. We don't mind working hard and being held accountable so long as we know the leader not only understands the mission but aligns and enlists us in the cause by appealing to our individual concerns, beliefs, and values.

[ ] Does not handicap us by hoarding information or by neglecting to ferret it out because of laziness, lack of curiosity, failure to network, or attempts at winning the Firefighters' Award for Quick-Fix Company A.

[ ] Always strives, despite forces and counterforces, to be fair.

[ ] Is open and vulnerable, not a shielded Attila battling an army of insecurities.

[ ] Listens empathetically by trying to find out first ''where each of us is coming from''; otherwise, buy-in of any request by the leader is likely to be half-hearted at best and the execution probably less than that.

[ ] Shirks doublespeak, smoke and mirrors, and similar turnoffs that, for a ''leader,'' are the kiss of death.

[ ] Provides structure and process so the strong are controlled and the weak are encouraged.

[ ] Balances freedom with discipline, knowing how long to fish (to analyze and ruminate) and when to cut bait (to be decisive).

[ ] Exhibits the kind of humility Isaac Newton exemplified when he said, "If I have seen further, it is by standing on the shoulders of giants."

[ ] Creates an environment where all of us feel comfortable to speak—where the messengers aren't killed with the messages.

[ ] Guides and teaches like a caring parent, giving us both roots and wings.

[ ] Celebrates our victories—small and large, individual and collective—and thus makes us eager to take the next step, to scale the next mountain.

Note: Consider turning the checklist into a survey. Have meeting members indicate your batting average in each case: 3 = Always, 2 = Quite Often, 1 = Sometimes, 0 = Never.

Associates and Suppliers

They share many of the attendees' expectations, but in addition they expect to be kept up to speed, to know what's happening and *why*. Curious creatures, they hunger for relevant information—especially if they know they'll have to come into the loop on a project at some time—and if the information flow is stifled by neglect or, worse yet, by intention, discontent can turn to hostility. From then on, a leader might just as well ask pigs to jig, cows to bow. Thus, when you call a meeting, make these assessments also:

• Which associates or suppliers, if any, might lend substance to this particular get-together? And how might that be accomplished without eating unnecessarily into people's time?

• In my conversations with associates, suppliers, and others, I've picked up hints as well as direct requests for information critical to their tasks and fundamental to the success of the matter I'm dealing with. Will this meeting be an appropriate vehicle for surfacing the information? If so, how can I bring it about?

• How do I plan to communicate the meeting outcomes pertaining to the work of these constituencies, especially those whose attendance is not yet needed?

LA ROSA: If you have good people, they're going to be curious and continue to be curious about how things work in terms of company decisions, operations, and so on. [In my own case] to withhold information from me denies me access to things that challenge me and let me grow. If I don't get it here long term, I'll just leave. If you're going to err, err on the side of telling me too much rather than telling me too little.

Customers

Regrettably, they are often left out of the equation when it comes to calling a meeting and meeting their expectations. An effective leader, however, pictures the customer—internal or external—as the primary attendee and, in planning the meeting, addresses the customer's pertinent questions. For example:

Queries from a Current Internal Customer

1. Why would I be pleased with the results of your meeting?

2. How is the meeting going to speed delivery or improve the quality of the product or service I need for my external customer?

3. If I could observe your group's get-together through a one-way mirror, why would I say to myself, "Nominate those people for a Baldrige Award"?

Queries from a Prospective External Customer

1. If I go with your company, ultimately I won't be buying a product or service as much as I'll be buying security, credibility, or similar expectations. Therefore, in the meeting you're calling, would I see such things being given a high priority?

2. In fact, is most of the meeting going to be about my interests and my concerns?

3. If I were to observe conflict in your meeting, would it be salutary, springing from disagreements on how to serve me best?

4. What do you plan on doing at the meeting to win me over—or to encourage my continuing interest in your organization?

Yourself

As Somerset Maugham once remarked, "If you refuse to accept anything but the best, you very often get it." And the meeting leaders who fail usually have expectations that rise to the level of mediocrity. Blaming and complaining replace personal responsibility and accountability. Excuse abuse ("I don't have time. . . . I wasn't hired for this. . . . And who cares anyway?") existed in the conference room long before it plagued today's judicial chambers.

But the respected leader, a person of quality and character, is mature enough not to succumb to such childish outlooks and laments. Unwilling to contribute to shoddy performance, the decline of an organization, or the tarnishing of their own reputations, respected leaders set measures for themselves that often exceed those of their followers. They know that the graphite in a No. 2 pencil also creates a diamond, but the latter, in its development, undergoes much greater pressure.

So whether they're calling a client or calling a meeting, these types of leaders never call quits to their own high standards and expectations. Neither should I. Neither should you.

Manager of Conversations and Commitments

Through the eyes of this character, each of us, in taking on the first responsibility, deals with:

- determining ways of bringing together interesting mixes of people for great sparks of ideas and flashes of discovery that ultimately benefit the customer and business
- finding ways to encourage give-and-take that gets beyond the superficial
- observing and responding to nonverbal language
- paying close attention to what's being said, why it's being said, and how it's being said—whether the words are spoken or written

Even more subtle, perhaps, is the need for:

- judging when best to say something to whom, where, when, why, and how while at the same time appreciating this piece of wisdom: "A closed mouth gathers no feet."

- monitoring turn-offs in your own inflections and body language
- knowing when to let silence punctuate a point
- being sure not to confuse a silenced person with a converted one
- sensing when the group has had enough dialogue to arrive at a consensus or when to retreat and cover former territory—perhaps from a completely different angle—because one or more participants are still having difficulty with understandings
- becoming more persistent and inquisitive so gains in confidence and knowledge can help in launching and probing controversial issues as well as enhancing the quality of decisions reached and tasks accomplished

Overcoming Resistance to Assignments

Getting people to commit to tasks and carry them out can be both formidable and frustrating. As someone said to me a few months ago, "When I go to a meeting, I have one objective and one objective only: to leave the meeting without an assignment." With all the meetings she was expected to attend and the additional responsibilities shoved onto her shoulders as a result of company cutbacks, evasion, to her, has become a coping mechanism.

The woman has countless sympathizers—and clones! That's why, in managing commitments, a meeting leader has to walk a fine line between getting the job done with the help of others and ensuring he or she isn't engendering resistance—for the kinds of reasons evidenced by this smattering of voices:

- *I haven't the foggiest idea why I'm sitting here in the first place.*
- *I fail to see the connection between what you're asking me to do and how it fits into the bigger picture.*
- *What's in it for me, anyway? Do I have a choice?*
- *I'm not sure you really know what you're after.*
- *You don't realize that what looks like a single task to you consists of many subordinate, time-consuming steps.*
- *I don't have the skill set to pull that off within the deadline you're expecting. I'm afraid to mention it, though, because you're likely to get irritated or lose faith in my capabilities.*

In those kinds of comments lie clues for you as a manager of commitments. Act on them.

1. Get to know, in your networks of relationships, as many as possible of the 20 percent of people you have to deal with 80 percent of the time. Find out what makes them tick, which skills they have, which skills they lack, what values they hold, and so on. Go to their workplaces, if possible. Invite them to yours. Or if distance is an issue, build profiles from the give-and-take of telephone conversations and similar exchanges. (Be curious, for heaven's sake!) Then, when it comes to approaching a person about tasks, the insights and rapport the two of you share are more likely to lead to commitments made *and* fulfilled.

> **HOWELL: When you have an employee who doesn't have to step up to special projects, in effect you're artificially rewarding the person by not putting extra work on him or her; you're not finding out what the person's true value (i.e., capability) is to the organization. . . . On the other hand, you shouldn't delegate something you don't continue to inspect. That is, you can't delegate unless you keep your eyes on it—not necessarily your hand, but your eyes.**

2. Realize that, in the frenzy of quick-fixes and seltzer bubbles of talk, a delegatee rarely gets a minute to clarify the purpose and scope of a task. In a hierarchical environment, failure to scope and clarify at the time a task is given and in the presence of others often leads underlings to do *more* than expected—just to cover their anatomies. If the pattern is allowed to persist (typically the case) people's resentments build, execution becomes erratic and sloppy, deadlines are missed, tempers flare, and whatever hopes exist for building team spirit are dashed or diminished.

3. Be sure the group sees the relevance and value of a task—that it's not just more pawing to satisfy the whimsy of Warthog:
   - *This will give us a chance to reduce the backlog.*
   - *Coming up with a contingency plan, Bibi, means no department will have to worry about a power failure.*

   By publicly stating benefits, you may find a participant has an even better, more efficient idea for achieving goals now that she or he is really tuned into the intent of the original task. Also, as an effective delegator, avoid the fate of the professor who shouts assignments over the clanging of the bell at the end of class and then grumbles about the terrible results. Instead, allow time in a meeting so you can take advantage of the next suggestion.

4. Screen commitments sounding like these:
   - *Will you do that, Fiona?*
   - *How about you, Jakeen?*
   - *Can you look into it, Meredith?*
   - Or a comment of this sort: *Okay, that'll be mine.*

Each shorthand comment assumes the assignment is clear, that the preceding discussion is understood by the intended delegatee. But if you were the delegator in any of the four situations—and wanted to get the commitment off to a good start—it would be wise to stop for a moment and check yourself:

   - Does Fiona interpret "that" to mean exactly what I mean?
   - Does Jakeen know precisely what I'm driving at? Can I assume he knows how to fill in the empty spaces with the right assignment?
   - Does "look into" connote the same intent and level of detail to Meredith as it does to me?
   - In the last sentence, what does the volunteer *really* mean? Does the comment mean what I infer? How can I be sure?

5. Provide leeway. Allow people to say "No" or "I'd like to pass on this one" or "What if I were to. . . ?" Don't scowl or howl. Listen and learn; be a wise old owl.

6. Don't rely on your memory to recall all the tasks doled out in Seltzerville. At a minimum, during the course of a meeting use an easel sheet or copyboard to fill in a matrix like this:

PERSON(S)   AGREED TO   SO THAT   BY THIS DATE

The most important column is labeled SO THAT. It forces the delegatee to face up to these questions instantly and publicly:

   - Why is the task being assigned?
   - Do I see how the task relates to our overall objective?

- Is the "agreed to" action likely to ensure the "so that"? If not, what adjustments might have to be made?
- Do I feel comfortable in my ability to handle the task now that I have a clear idea of what it is?

Finally, use the matrix to see that tasks are shared equally and fairly, to note where you may need to lower political barriers, defuse land mines, or the like. The device can help you monitor follow-up conversations, depending on a delegatee's familiarity with a task, skill level, and degree of freedom desired in choosing how to complete an assignment. Limited publication and distribution of the matrix can also keep nosy JIC-Ps from swelling subsequent get-togethers, particularly those satisfied by knowing the *whys* of the *whats*.

7. Lower resistance to a task by inviting two or three people to share it.

8. Be available. Don't vanish altogether. Use your antennae to know when to follow up and when to back off.

9. Don't expect others to do what you wouldn't do yourself. In the game of leadership, wimps never win.

10. Keep your eyes open and your ears to the ground. Don't panic the moment you hear something's amiss. Don't meddle, either. But do keep in touch with what's happening, so when individuals make certain discoveries affecting the tasks of others—an inevitability—you can help manage, if need be, the accuracy and specificity of the conversations and commitments dealing with the ripples.

General Contractor

Anticipate, plan, and communicate like a general contractor, the person who oversees that construction project on the interstate. He or she has a master plan—a vision—shared with all the subcontractors. So even though they may seem to be acting willy nilly as we drive by, each has a clear sense of what's to be done, when, and why, but *how* things are done is left to the individual workers exercising their expertise. Eventually, of course, the vision is realized, the alignment of tasks has paid off, and we share vicariously in the marvel and accomplishment.

Anticipate, plan, and communicate. Anticipate, plan, and communicate. Those skills of the master contractor are also keys to successful meeting leadership. Let them pound in your brain with a jackhammer's unretreating, repeating beat.

CAMERON: In Mission Control (what you see on TV), each one of those consoles is supported by a small group of people in a back room looking directly at telemetrics. The guys in Mission Control are all wearing headsets, listening to the flight crew, listening to the flight director on a different audio system, and listening to their own back room. They're also constantly evaluating their own system on the one hand and trying to get a feel for the overall mission: How does their particular system affect everything else that's going on? Besides that, they're trying to look ahead to see what's the next problem. If they have a new problem on top of what they've already got, how does that fit in?

Symphonic Conductor

The role of conductor is perhaps one of the more obvious when it comes to leading a group of individuals so they create something greater than themselves. Often overlooked, however, are these more subtle and equally important skills:

1. Knowing when to cue in certain individuals at the right time so themes are played to completion without interruption.

One of the easiest ways to facilitate this task, I have found, is to require meeting participants to raise their hands when they want to talk. When they signal, I quickly write down their names or initials on a pad, or have a committee member keep track. For example, Lee might be the first to raise her hand and speak. While she's making her point, three others have thoughts jogged loose. They simply raise their hands or arch their eyebrows as I nod and note their names; the actions are unobtrusive.

M.C.
Caitlin
Jo

After Lee has spoken, I will ask, "Who wants to follow that thread?" M.C. may say he does, and then speaks to the point. Caitlin, when it comes her turn, may say, "Pass. I have a different thread." And then Jo takes up the thread Lee started. When Jo finishes—and her name is crossed off the list—I may go next to Alex, who was prompted into action by something Jo mentioned:

~~M.C.~~
Caitlin
~~Jo~~
Alex

After Alex completes his message, I may say something to this effect: "Is there anyone else who wants to continue the thread? [PAUSE] If not, then Caitlin is going to switch to a brand new thought." [PAUSE for the group to shift its collective gear]. "Go ahead, Caitlin."

At that point, Caitlin may trigger a give-and-take with Tyler. Constantly observing the group's reaction, I let the two go back and forth ("Continue the discourse," I say) until the dialogue reaches it natural conclusion—usually after three or four exchanges—or until it needs to be taken offline because of its level of detail or because a tangent threatens the main focus.

Now and then I will mention who's in the loop, or queue, so all know they will be heard and won't be left vying for attention in a cacophony of shouts or the discords of tangential topics that lead to the fat and chaos of meeting melees. (*Note:* Names might be listed on an easel sheet to negate the need for periodic announcements.)

As the meeting is conducted this way, participants soon find themselves avoiding the repetition of a point ("Take me off the list"), speaking concisely when they know others are awaiting their turns ("I'll be brief"), judging whether it's worth pursuing another sub-theme ("Hmm . . . let me think some more . . . pass"), jotting an idea on an index card, realizing a whole new issue needs to be addressed later on ("I think we should add this question to the Issues Easel Sheet"), and checkpointing certain messages and inferences ("Before I go on, Lee, here's what I heard you say. . . . ").

A variation on the dialectic might include these prompts and reactions:

- *"Who agrees with Caitlin's point and would like to pursue it?"* [PAUSE: Allow for responses from the hand-signalers.]
- *"Who disagrees with Caitlin's point and would like to speak?"* [PAUSE]. *"Hmm . . . I assume silence signals the group's agreement?"* [PAUSE: Allow for responses if the assumption pricks someone into speaking.]

The process, though it takes a few minutes to explain here, actually runs smoothly and quickly. What's more, its benefits are significant. It gives structure to the meeting, forces people to be better listeners, encourages them to judge the value and importance of intended comments, controls those who may have tended to dominate, frees those who might have been muted, prevents the intrusion of tangents, and allows clarity to grow as participants hear the emphases of leitmotifs drumrolling to understandings and closure.

2. Hearing slight dissonance.

Was that an undertone of discontent? Did that last comment signal doubt? Am I hearing the word *won't* a bit too often? An effective meeting leader tunes in; detects the notes of concern, confusion, or doubt, and acts upon them—perhaps then and there or during an extended break:

- *Are you uncomfortable with something, Jim?*
- *In the discussion on digital imaging, Amy, when you said, "I've heard all that before," I gathered you might be frustrated or skeptical. Is there any particular reason?*

As you pick up on dissonance, find out—by lending an empathetic ear—where a member's struggle is really coming from, building on the chords of responses your interplay evokes.

3. Getting the strings to stretch.

When strings are not stretched, the instruments and players are worthless. It's getting them to stretch (to high standards) and expecting sections to bow in unison, or alignment—without breaking the strings—that produces the music, that gets the meeting singing.

4. Being extremely sensitive to pace and rhythm, timing and momentum.

It's important as a meeting leader to understand the music of the business.

For there's a rhythm and pace to an effective agenda. There's a good time and a bad time to bring in the silent one, to call for a caucus or breakout groups, to recap. There are also giant sweeps and repeats of movements in a collaborative meeting—from congregating, affiliating, and educating to deliberating, negotiating, and consummating. And there's the need to appreciate the momentum of a truly substantive, decision-making discussion and to ensure its quickening, uninterrupted pace as it builds into the final crescendos of an *1812 Overture.*

Psychologist

It doesn't take Psychology 101 to figure out that if you kill the messenger with the message, you'll be waiting till doomsday before you get timely but negative information again. Yet that kind of stupidity—and arrogance—ruins the effectiveness of many a leader. That's why it's important to monitor the dynamics of a group. In each category that follows, for example, sense when it's wise to implement a suggestion.

> **". . . I feel that the two rhythms are entirely different things. I mean the rhythm and pace of action and pace of dialogue. The problem is to try and blend these two things together."**
>
> *Alfred Hitchcock,*
> *Film Director*

1. Dealing with the agenda:
   - Forget what the clock reads and let debate continue.
   - Replace an agenda altogether because discoveries early in a session signal the group's need and desire to pursue more worthwhile matters.

- Lift up on the table an issue being danced around, perhaps taking advantage of the "surprise" to surface what lies at the heart of the matter before extending deliberation—if the group prefers—to the next meeting when everyone's had a chance to reflect.
- Adjourn earlier than scheduled, especially if tensions are high and emotional distancing needs to occur before the group reconvenes.

> YANG: Sometimes you have to change an agenda midstream rather than stick to whatever you've planned. If it's wrong, then scrap it. Redesign it right then. If you stick too closely to an agenda, you won't get at some of the real issues.

2. Handling certain participant behaviors:
   - Show a brief video that satirizes certain meeting or business behaviors.
   - Allow a person to release steam, after which you might kiddingly say, "Well, would you care to tell us how you *really* feel?"
   - Comment on a behavior you'd like others to model.
   - Give well-earned public praise for an individual's insight without alienating those who might be seeking your approval as well.
   - Offer a face-saving escape route to someone whose arguments may have unwittingly boxed him or her in.
   - Question specifically, firmly, and completely a naysayer, a backbiter, or any of their cousins.
   - Let a person enjoy a well-deserved laugh, a spontaneous round of applause, or some other moment in the spotlight.

3. Assessing your own behaviors:
   - Make a quick, on-the-spot assessment of what might be your own counterproductive behaviors.
   - Give in on a point of little or no consequence to you.
   - Admit a *mea culpa*, a goof-up.

4. Minding the momentum:
   - Pose a closed question, one that can be answered yes or no, rather than an open-ended one demanding explanation.
   - Seek feedback from junior-ranking or introverted individuals before calling on senior-ranking or extroverted participants.
   - Include adversaries on an assignment in the same small breakout group, so public posturings and grandstandings are minimized and differences can be settled in a more private give-and-take.
   - Remain silent with everyone else, rather than fill the void with a segue of aimless patter.

- Push through to a group's decision so as not to allow participants' subsequent doubts or their colleagues' ridicule of the decision to cause revisits and reversals.
- Celebrate major milestones.

Humorist

"He who laughs, lasts," said Robert Fulghum, author of *All I Really Need to Know I Learned in Kindergarten*. And in the meeting room, especially one rife with tension, humorous relief is essential and salutary.

A spontaneous piece of wit, a well-timed pause followed by a deadpan rebuttal, a cartoon flashed on the screen, or whatever seems naturally amusing and right to you can enliven a group. So don't be afraid to loosen up, to reveal a lighter side (assuming you have one!), and to poke fun at your own foibles, which are not to be confused with a great set of scruples.

Don't, however, turn the meeting into Comedy Central. Balance is the key. Being able to launch a good laugh or to be the brunt of one, even while carrying on the serious matters of business, brings to mind this piece of wisdom from the dramatist James Barrie: "The secret of happiness is not in doing what one likes, but in liking what one does." In committee work, that message infects and inspires.

> "For goodness' sake," said Mother Crab to her daughter, "why don't you walk like other creatures instead of crawling backwards in that ridiculous fashion!"
>
> "I would if I could," replied the daughter, "but all I learned about walking I learned from you."
>
> *Aesop*

Historian and Storyteller

What is the history of your organization? Who were some standouts who left their marks on it? What are the memorable tales that reveal the company's character and image? Moreover, how do all those things fit into the matter of the day, and why should anyone care?

Employees who live in a highly transient culture may not always know or appreciate the answers, the traditions they're expected to uphold. They may not be aware of the failures and successes that have led to the moment at hand, nor how dealing with it efficiently and effectively might add to the organization's luster.

Therefore, by digging into the past, respecting it, and connecting it to those in the present—through offline bits of chit-chat or well-timed anecdotes in the midst of give-and-take—you can infuse followers with not only a sense of commitment to the company and customer but also an impetus to "Let's get with it," the attitude ensuring a bright and prosperous future.

8

schizophrenic cabbage?

Turning participants on—from fishing for the right mix to storyboarding and document-making

Their faces flash across the TV screen. Ears cupped by headsets, most of the people sit fixed in concentration. Occasionally the camera cuts to a pair arched over their desks in animated talk, their thoughts prompted, perhaps, by the speaker, who's wearing a djellabah. Oblivious to everything, as the camera lingers on him, is a full-bellied delegate—sound asleep, mouth open, headset askew. Engraved nameplates tell the rest of the story: Azerbaijan, Greece, Belize, Zaire, and nearly 180 others glimpsed in a pull-back view of the room. It's a meeting of the U.N. General Assembly, hastily gathered by a crisis of international proportion.

Not much different, is it, from scenes multiplied hundreds of thousands of times each day in meeting rooms everywhere. A crisis triggers a powwow. People from all corners of the company (or department) assemble, bringing with them an array of personal backgrounds and professional experiences as well as expectations, concerns, and vested interests. Headsets and nameplates are not in sight, but such devices might serve the meeting well, for the representatives also speak the unique languages of their homelands, be it R&D, Manufacturing, Sales/Marketing, Finance, Human Resources, Distribution, or, at times, the paramilitaristic dialects of such island nations as Security and Facilities Planning.

Meeting outcomes depend, to a large extent, on how well leaders recognize, respect, and manage those kinds of differences by controlling process and thus participants. As we all know, having sat among the huddled masses, the challenges are demanding. Even the leader Jesus said centuries ago, "If a house be divided against itself, that house cannot stand." A leader needs followers; followers need a leader. And in collaborative meetings particularly, their symbiosis—or lack of it—can indeed make the difference between houses that stand and those that crumble.

THE BOTHERED AND BEWILDERING

Participants are a complicated lot. They evidence attitudes that, at times, seem downright schizophrenic. In my workshop surveys, for example, they complain about finding meetings frustrating if not intolerable for the following reasons:

- no agenda
- spineless or unprepared leaders
- topics irrelevant to the participants' individual responsibilities
- too many tangents
- domination by a few participants
- disappointment with their own inability to contribute
- interruptions when they do try to say something
- too many side discussions
- a tendency to drag on or ooze from one meeting to another like egg yolks in a fry pan
- lack of clarity about outcomes

Large numbers of respondents also report they become angry, resistant, or totally turned off when they:

- feel as if they seldom matter
- hunger for fast results but have to suffer the chicken pluckers

- feel rushed or bamboozled by the firefighting Type A's
- are blindsided or manipulated by devious bosses
- have to bite their tongues when others "*still* aren't getting it!"
- have no means for expressing themselves without "looking foolish"
- want closure on a talked-to-death topic before they leap across the table and strangle the compulsive yakkers

Despite such complaints, I've observed that many of these same people, whose counterparts must litter the corporate landscape, act like meeting groupies. They exercise little or no judgment about which get-togethers to attend and holler loudest whenever they're left out of a loop. What's more, they avoid assignments, show reluctance to commit to a decision, exhibit arrested adolescent behaviors they themselves wouldn't tolerate, and, like the "spineless wimps" they chastise, sit in bunches—like cabbages—doing nothing about the runaway engine or Galapagos turtle. Why? To a person, the answer is virtually the same: "It's not *my* meeting!"

Therein lies the problem.

Is It Any Wonder Confusion Reigns?

Most participants don't view their get-togethers as "*our* meetings." It's Joe's or Judy's meeting, Mr. Ramon's, or the VP's. I've aided and abetted that attitude myself; you probably have too. We do it in any number of ways, even if unwittingly.

In our rush, perhaps we become heavy-handed about "running the show." Perhaps we fail to involve others in planning meetings, if we plan at all. Perhaps we forsake issues after declaring them top priority. Perhaps we shift priorities with channel-surfing abandon. Or perhaps we betray our interest in the customer and business by speaking more often about "What I want," "What I need," and "What I think we ought to do." If we combine those kinds of lapses with the litany of complaints above, is it any wonder participants become confused, passive, resistant, or ultimately alienated? Of course not.

> **FINCH: There's an image of the authoritarian military leader who has all the answers, makes all the key decisions, conducts the briefings at the map, and tells people to "Charge!" But the most successful leaders I've seen have been very collaborative, have allowed a great deal of give-and-take, and have been particularly good at having contrary opinions voiced.**

Full Engagement Is Key

This book aims to help you to change that situation. In fact, you already may have begun to jettison chunks of lard, discarding the kinds of waste that occur with dog-and-pony shows, long distribution lists, and e-mail mayhem. Those tactics, plus others suggested in Part I, provide an important start to maintaining a diet of fat reduction and revitalization.

Building on those slim-trimmers, which helps "free up" time for the really important things, this chapter shows how to begin achieving high participation in collaborative meetings by using techniques that purposefully involve members and *keep* them involved. For no matter the outcome of a meeting, it's only as good as the degree of commitment given to it. Therefore, participants must feel they've been heard and understood. Their full engagement is key.

FISHING FOR THE RIGHT MIX

It bears repeating: If you don't take time to know the individuals on your task force or committee—and for them to know each other—you make work longer and harder for all. If, for instance, you only know Mallory Hamilton is from accounting or Harvey Dumont "does something over there in manufacturing," you might just as well talk to monkey wrenches.

It's knowing your members as unique human beings that enables you to appeal to their individual wants and needs, their values, their concerns, their beliefs. Without that type of information, plus some familiarity with members' occupational dialects, trying to build understandings and reach consensus can be as hopeless as trying to tack Jell-O on the wall.

Believe you me, when those U.N. representatives aren't sitting in the assembly, they're spending hours and hours getting to know their allies as well as their adversaries—from "official" vs. "personal" political stances right down to wine preferences. In corporate America, that kind of research is usually limited to the sales department and boardrooms—boundaries that mindsets and mavericks must learn to hurdle.

Avoiding Deadbeats

Getting the right representatives on a committee—preferably four to seven members and no more than ten—often determines your chances for success. But you can't expect much when you troll with an announcement like this:

It's been determined that facility needs at Danzing have to be looked into. To that end, a task force is being formed that will have its first meeting on May 3. Please submit to me the name and address of your department's representative.

The law of averages says you'll reel in some winners, but you're absolutely assured of hooking some dead fish and a waterlogged boot or two. They are:

- the first person a delegator thinks of, who happens to have about as much interest in the project as a cadaver does in caskets

- the ruthless servant of some remotely familiar delegator who, jealously guarding his or her turf, drools at the prospect of doing you in

- an annoying or mean-spirited employee whom a delegator ships to your task force, hoping it's the next best thing to a Siberian gulag

- an employee chosen by the delegator because serving on the task force will represent a "developmental opportunity" for him or her; but the delegator warns you not

- someone who's delighted to fly in for your powwow so she or he can squeeze in a visit with the sibling of the spouse's third cousin, twice removed

Naturally, you can't avoid those characters altogether. In fact, on occasion they turn out to be enjoyable surprises. Still, you're taking an enormous risk, especially if you have much to accomplish in a short period.

PEEPLES: Choose your participants wisely—that's the number one ingredient for a fat-free meeting.

Think how helpful it would be to call or walk to the offices of potential delegators whom you've gotten to know and with whom you can speak openly about the specific problem to be solved, the potential benefits in doing so, and which representative in each case might serve the cause well. How much better that would be than dashing off a missive like the preceding and being saddled with one person after another, including a last-minute draftee who has neither the skill set nor desire to participate—a reason for many meeting failures.

When distance has to be spanned by online capabilities, consider adapting the All-Purpose Request shown on page 94. Help all delegators make well-informed choices, saving you the anchors of seaweed and blubbery rubber.

Seek Diversity, Nip Oversights

Whenever possible, seek diversity. Assemble your own mini U.N. of talent, representing different functions, experiences, backgrounds, points of view, temperaments, and so on. If you go for only a bunch of cookie-cutter lackeys, you won't generate the flint of debate necessary for real breakthroughs.

YANG: I try to ensure that the right people are in the room, which means people with knowledge of the subject as well as people who have the authority to make the decision. The problem is when you have either too many people or the wrong people. If you have the right people there in the smallest possible number, you're more likely to have an efficient meeting.

DUENOW: There's a fine line between having the right people and the right number of people in decision making—especially in a bureaucracy.

One way to ensure diversity—and to avoid overlooking a critically important player—is to have a list of departments or functions available to pull up on screen or glance at on an office bulletin board. Or it sometime helps to flip through your organization's phone directory, noting departmental designations. As you think about your project, note the entries and ask, *If I were performing that function, why might I have an interest in the task force topic?*

By not doing something like that, a group in a California company squandered days. They were trying to figure how to make their user manuals more effective. It wasn't until several meetings into the effort that someone pointed out that Kyoko, the company's graphic designer, might be able to help. Hardly anyone knew her except through her "nifty little brochures." What a surprise they got when she was invited and began to share her thoughts and sketches. Result: The meetings buzzed along with a renewed energy, the manuals achieved a user-friendly design later commended by customers, and, for

REQUEST FOR REPRESENTATION ON A TASK FORCE

Date: April 11, 19—

To: All Department Heads

Re: Appointing a Representative to Serve on a Facilities Planning Task Force

Background: Because of the increase in the employee population, Herlihy Ltd. plans to move from the Danzing site. Right now we have 560 employees squeezed into offices originally built to accommodate 300. New facilities should have expansion capabilities for an employee base of 1200.

Purpose/Scope: The task force, consisting of nine members, is to:

1. determine the best site within a 50-mile radius of Danzing
2. establish criteria for a "best site"
3. determine the pros and cons of each site considered

Limitations: The scope of the work will *not* involve discussions with city officials or inspections of any buildings.

Deliverables: The committee is to submit recommendations to the Executive Board, with appropriate maps and a matrix of advantages and disadvantages of each site.

Your Candidate: For your department to achieve maximum benefit from the effort, please appoint a representative who:

1. has a genuine interest in the topic, since decisions will affect your logistical concerns
2. is familiar with the geography of the Danzing area, including major highways and access to public transportation

Duration: The task force will begin May 6 and end June 10.

Deadline: I'd appreciate the name of your representative, plus e-mail address, no later than April 25. Many thanks.

ultimately saving the company tens of thousands of dollars on outsourcing, Kyoko won a distinguished-employee award.

As this incident shows, bringing in an "outsider" can affect the dynamics of a group, redirect their perspectives, and give them a recharge. Calculating for that effect by inviting an engineer to a sales meeting, a retail customer to a design powwow, and so on can do wonders—from offering a refreshing but unbiased point of view, which is a time-saver in disguise, to putting smiles on those who might otherwise exercise their glower power.

NELSON: We're trying to get people to think boundaryless. That means if I am going to design a product, what I need to do is put together a cross-functional team so we can start working the process from the get-go and maybe identify some of the issues we're going to have in the different departments. Our old philosophy was to design it in engineering and throw it over the wall to manufacturing and then over the wall to sales, and so on. Now we start with finding out what's important to the customer and work back from that.

Checking Comfort Levels

After the first two or three sessions of a long-term, cross-functional task force or similar group, hold a checkpoint. Get a reading on the comfort level of participants, especially last-minute draftees. It's an important part of managing expectations as well as conversations and commitments.

Meet one-on-one with the team members, request they meet with their delegators, or do both. If you choose to involve each delegator, which is almost always a good idea, you may want to vary the following request:

Getting Your Delegatee's Perspective

To make sure Keegan Sinclair feels the task force on [TOPIC] is likely to benefit him, and he's likely to benefit it, would you please spend a few minutes with Keegan next week to get a reading? I'd appreciate it.

I hope he's finding the project worthwhile, but if he's not, Chris, please consider appointing a replacement. It would be unfair to

Keegan, other participants, and perhaps your department to have his reluctant involvement affect the team's progress and outcomes.

All team members have agreed to this checkpoint and understand the reason for it. Though many members have been vocal about how we can improve the effort, the checkpoint may give a face-saving out to any member with minimal or no interest.

Thanks, Chris, for helping in the success of the group's work. I'll be happy to return the favor.

Now, before you think "Who's got time for that?" think about this: Who has time to play social worker with a participant feeling shanghaied? Who has time to be ball-and-chained by a polar-cap exile or some other delegator's personnel problem, a person who should be handled compassionately by a specialist? Who has time to coddle a participant who'd rather be somewhere else and would love to tell you in no uncertain terms but isn't given a chance?

PEEPLES: If people don't participate after two meetings on a task force, I meet with them individually and ask, Do you really think this group is helping you in any way? Are you getting any benefit? If they aren't benefiting, they should be allowed to leave in a graceful way. By the same token, I've had to pull out people who were arrogant or highly negative and tell them, "Obviously we can't meet your needs. So there's no point in our wasting your time any further."

In those kinds of cases, playing goodie two-shoes produces chronically painful feet. And with all the other things demanding your attention—not the least of which is ensuring results to maintain your group's dynamism and membership—you certainly have no time for whirlpools and bunion rubs!

Self-Assessment of Meeting Behaviors

Before each meeting ends, be sure to have members fill out an evaluation form like that shown on page 60. The tool provides you with not only insights and tips for adjusting your meetings but also a motivating mechanism that says to members, *Your feedback is important to our success. We're not here just to while away time.*

Also, feedback from the form on page 98 might help you further. It shortcuts discoveries that might take too long for your antennae to detect. Completing it also allows members to reflect on behaviors they may never have examined but may want to change or manage better, to their advantage and that of colleagues.

SQUARES AND CHAIRS?
A HARD LOOK AT SEATING

Where Pearl and Earl sit might make or break a meeting, for seating arrangements are vital to group dynamics. The theater style of the U.N. General Assembly, for example, produces an effect different from the circular table around which the 15 members of the Security Council sit. Recall, also, the TV shots of the Oval Office, a semicircular panel in a congressional hearing room, or the solid, square negotiation table inside the perimeter of an outer square that serves the aides of the mayor and union officials.

In Paris in 1969, before the Vietnam peace talks began, weeks were spent determining table shape and seating. In business meetings, however, we barely give such matters an eyeblink. As a result, a confrontational atmosphere is aggravated by "all of them" sitting opposite "all of us." Or the Bobbsie Twins sit and chat off and on, off and on, while high-ranking enemies duke it out with glares across the way, ghettos remain intact, and quiet church mice and the minorities get shunted to the side. Then we wonder, *Why didn't the meeting go so well?*

That question often baffled Chuck, a vice president who would helicopter from his Southwest headquarters to a subsidiary, give a 45-minute overhead presentation to 80 or 90 in a mini-theater, and then feel puzzled by the lack of questions from his anesthetized audience—employees with whom he wanted to develop some camaraderie. Though brilliant in many ways, Chuck never thought of holding the meeting in the cafeteria and using the circular tables for "buzz groups." Or giving the employees a rundown of topics and allowing them to confer among themselves before responding to him and interacting with him on key issues raised during a ten-minute briefing.

Controlling the meeting process, and thereby the participants, calls, in part, for playing at least two of a leader's roles: host and psychologist. From those perspectives, ask yourself the following questions and then decide which arrangement might serve the meeting best:

WHAT ARE YOUR PREFERENCES AND NEEDS?

So I can be aware of certain of your preferences and attitudes, and try to accommodate them in planning and leading our meetings, please complete the statements below. Your honest answers will help benefit everyone, including you.

1. I like to prepare for a meeting by doing the following: _____
   _____.

2. Before reading advanced materials for a meeting, I need to hear, see, or feel that _____
   because _____.

3. When things are going well in a meeting, I tend to show my satisfaction by _____.

4. When things are NOT going well in a meeting, I usually _____
   _____
   because I have a need to _____.

5. In problemsolving and decision making, I need to _____
   _____.

6. I prefer to do the following in a meeting: [ ] share my thoughts out loud OR [ ] listen, reflect, and then perhaps speak.

7. If I feel I'm NOT being heard in a meeting or given a chance to get involved, I tend to _____.

8. I am most eager to accept an assignment when _____
   _____.

9. I begin feeling like part of a well-oiled machine when I _____
   _____.

10. When I say a meeting was terrific, I often mean that in terms of my needs, it _____.

- As I think about the objectives of the meeting, should I consider a setting different from the conventional meeting room?
- To what extent will the shape of the table(s), the placement of screen(s), and so on constrain the interaction? How might I circumvent the limitations?
- Whom might I separate—or put near each other—because they represent similar areas of expertise or share a reporting relationship?
- Which side-by-side or face-to-face seats might allow relative strangers, such as client and supplier, to get to know each other?
- Who should probably be separated so eye contact is minimal or impossible?
- Can I discourage an infamous monopolizer or intimidator by placing him or her off to the side, squeezed between a couple of beefy fullbacks?
- Is this a time to put adversaries right next to each other so they'll have to confer during certain periods of the meeting?
- How might the head, foot, or center of a long rectangle allow a shrinking violet to flourish?

Be discerning, of course. Among four or five intimates, seating may not be an issue. But for the dynamics you want to achieve among a larger number, you may have to alter the pattern of a current, familiar group by resorting to agenda sheets and index-card designators (see pages 34–35). Or to establish the expectations of six or more participants convening for the first time, you may want to indicate specific seats with name tents. Nevertheless, considering seating arrangements as part of facilitating a collaborative meeting brings you to this fork in the road: Either you value attention to detail or court disaster. The choice is yours.

WALTON: Taping name tags to tables can be critical. It signals that the meeting has a structure, a plan. Once people accept the structure, they find freedom.

PLAYING BY THE GROUND RULES

After assembling the right mix of people and figuring out which seating configuration might work best for their interaction, help them determine a set of ground rules to operate by. Sometimes called a meeting contract or agreement, a set of simple guidelines can do for a small, collaborative group what Robert's Rules do for a large, deliberative body. They provide a structure—an order—that *frees* people; without it, turmoil is virtually guaranteed.

The rules are stoplights at a four-way intersection. When they're working, traffic flows smoothly. But when the beacons are out, what a difference: Either it's every car for itself or it's a do-si-do routine bollixed up by drivers unaware of the pattern or acting in selfish disregard of it. Tempers flare. Horns honk. Chaos reigns.

To prevent those kinds of behaviors in meetings, bring up the need for, and benefits of, ground rules. Then encourage members to agree on five to seven entries. Following, for example, are ground rules often used by groups with which I work at GTE. The set represents a single investment of a few hours, but its repeated use has paid handsomely—and continues to do so—in sapping the fat.

We agree to . . .

1. Stick to the agenda, beginning and ending on time.

2. Let each person speak without interruption, unless the interruption is to raise a point of order or to clarify a point.

3. Stay to the end of the meeting, and not come and go at will. *Note:* If someone has to come and go, then it will be the person's responsibility to keep up to speed. There will be no revisiting of items to accommodate the come-and-goer, and neither will his or her absence be allowed to impede the group's progress.

4. Welcome conflict, but keep personalities out of the dialogue.

5. Guard against voice inflections that may indicate disdain, impatience, or other counterproductive attitudes.

6. Share in accepting assignments.

7. Make decisions and commit to them.

Posting the ground rules high on a wall, and keeping them there for all to glimpse from time to time, allows you as a leader to:

- Cite an entry in the *group's* contract when there's an infraction, thus cushioning you from being viewed or attacked as the heavy. For example: "Excuse me, Blair, we agreed not to interrupt. Why not jot down your thought on an index card, and I'll come back to you." *Note:* You'll have to screw up your courage only a couple of times to make the comment before a Blair or others take to the hint and a new habit.

- Use the agreement in combination with references to time (thanks to the clock), slim-trimmers involving the 3 × 5, and the follow-the-thread procedure described on pages 81–84. Together they help you facilitate the give-and-take while also controlling behaviors of those who tend to run an intersection or slam-brake at dead center.

By leaving the rules posted, you can also encourage their implementation among other groups using the room. Finally, boxing or highlighting a set of agreed-to ground rules on agendas for teleconferences can turn hollering contests into reasonably pleasant dinnertime conversations.

Once you begin adhering to the ground rules and appealing to a sense of fairness, you'll hardly ever have to refer to the entries among the same people. As with any rules of a game frequently played and enjoyed, they become internalized—so much so, in fact, that participants begin kidding around with them (for example, paying a hefty $1 fine anytime Rule 5 is broken).

Without rules of play, however, there is no game, there is no fun. For in abiding by their covenant with one another, participants realize how it frees them in ways many of them haven't experienced before. What an empowering and impelling force that is!

STORYBOARDING THE OUTPUT

Most task forces or committees issue interim reports, final reports, or both. The participating collaborators don't simply convene to exchange ideas; they meet to produce documents. If you and committee members approach the experience from that angle, collaborative get-togethers become more action-oriented and intellectually stimulating.

One way to ensure the document-making perspective is to start with a storyboard, using 5 × 8 index cards. After timing its use repeatedly, I've found that, whenever possible, posting a tentative sequence of "topic cards" either before or at the beginning of a meeting works best, even if the whole kit and caboodle gets tossed later as a result of discoveries. Here are the motivating pluses of storyboarding, whether a committee's task lasts for a single, intensive day or stretches over weeks:

- Based on cues from a group's charter, a storyboard provides a mechanism for taking an important preliminary look at a deliverable from the moment it seems appropriate to do so. If a group has no charter, then storyboarding helps set, at an early stage, a focus that may be desperately wanting, fat-threatening, or both.

  Note: If you can afford the time and believe it will benefit a group's esprit de corps, have participants suggest tentative topics during a brainstorm following exploratory deliberations; from the suggestions, sequence a tentative table of contents, i.e., storyboard. Another option is to post one yourself or invite a "giraffe" of a member to stick his or her neck out. A rough cut usually takes only a few minutes.

- In restating and clarifying the objectives of a meeting, a storyboard helps "tangibilitate" the amount of work the group may have to tackle, depending on how the cards are rearranged as the meeting evolves.

- Determining the prospective primary audience, plus other readers, if any, not only affects the storyboard contents but helps participants adjust whatever myopic viewpoints they may have brought with them. In other words, they begin realizing they haven't convened simply to engage in a self-serving exercise. The storyboard—color-coded, if possible, with names of the "story's" prospective readers above it—keeps committee members alert to their ultimate task. Thus, the device becomes an aligning vehicle as well as the group's conscience.

- When they estimate the amount of writing and illustrating they may have to do (everyone gets involved eventually), participants begin to consider the deadline, note the agenda and clock, and consciously or unconsciously think about how they're going to act and what they're going to contribute now that the storyboard helps guide relevance. Also, cooperation and teaming are more often the rule than not, mainly because of the next point.

- As deliberation, sketching, and so on lead to the Ahas! of shared understandings, participants add, delete, resequence, or combine parts of the storyboard—a major initial step in producing their common document. The process, detailed in Chapter 15 on group writing, taps into every human being's deep-seated, psychological need to make something, to create order out of chaos. And because of that universal impulse, even participants who at first show signs of reluctance begin to enjoy tackling the challenge, as long as results keep reflecting individuals' valued contributions and the group's consensus about a subject of importance to them and their prospective readers. In sum, the compelling motivation for participants comes from knowing that in starting with a storyboard, they'll give birth to a document they'll ultimately shape, sign, publish, and distribute. From that process springs synergy, commitment, and pride in ownership.

ENGAGING "THE QUIET ONES"

> "What a person really fears is not so much extinction but extinction with insignificance."
>
> *Ernest Becker*
> *Anthropologist*

As you've probably gathered by now, the type of participant who often concerns and irritates leaders is the person who sits and says nothing—meeting after meeting after meeting. In fact, it is this number-one Least Wanted character who invariably galvanizes debate in my workshops.

Before looking at how "process" can help a leader deal with the challenge of the silent ones, consider just a few of the possible reasons for their silence:

- They're introverted types who may be doing much more thinking and reflecting than the kennel yippers.
- Like many who may have been traumatized by the shushers and hushers of classroom years, they have laliophobia, the fear of public speaking.
- The topic of the meeting—or moment—holds no interest.
- As last-minute appointees told to "Get there pronto!" they spend most of their time trying to figure out the lay of the land and language.
- The leader, who's a Type A dynamo, defers to his or her clones in the meeting, thus driving seething introverts into stony defiance.

- Not having been supplied an agenda or reluctant to ask for one, they prefer risking silence to the vulnerability of ill-preparedness.
- They may come from ethnic backgrounds in which "a nail that pops up gets hammered down"; that is, calling attention to oneself is considered rude or impolite.
- They are dependent, rebellious self-haters, who, according to psychiatrist Theodore Isaac Rubin, "cannot make a decision until someone else makes it, so they know which road is the opposite to take."

Seat-warmers of the last type should not, of course, be tolerated; give 'em the boot! Others, however, who are quiet and retiring but have contributions to make must be encouraged in ways that are comfortable for them. Without the buy-in of all participants in one form or another, the quality of a decision and commitment is seriously jeopardized. So, too, are the clarity and persuasiveness of the document explaining the outcomes on which others are expected to act. That's why it's helpful to use the following guidelines from Richard C. Maybury, an authority on organizational development and human behavior:

Appealing to Let-Us-Think, Inc.

1. Provide introverts with an agenda and reading materials ahead of time.

2. When critical decisions need to be made, use the first meeting to provide all data and an outline of the issues to be decided. Then schedule a second meeting to make the decisions.

3. Encourage the introverts to speak first and last at a meeting, but don't pressure them.

4. Consider setting a ground rule stating that discussions or decisions cannot be made outside the meeting; introverts will defer to that if allowed.

5. Provide all the data early in the meeting, allowing the extroverts to question, debate, and be cathartic. Then ask the introverts their perspectives without interrupting.

6. Coax out details—through matter-of-fact questioning—to understand the introverts, to whom talking is energy-draining.

7. Include opportunities for introverts to put their thoughts and positions in writing, to be shared with the group before a meeting is held.

Keep remembering, as well, that with many, if not most, collaborative efforts:

1. The group is creating a document.

2. Creating the document may occur in stages represented by a series of meetings.

3. Everyone should be encouraged to contribute to the process; otherwise, idle hands and minds become the devil's workshop.

Assigning roles to participants—ahead of time or on the spot—helps them realize they're not on a cruise at the company's expense while you steer the ship, load the cargo, tend the engines, cook the meals, and deejay the dance-off. It's their journey, too. And among the positions they might be asked to take are:

Scribe-on-Call. Never knowing when the need will arise or when you'll give a nod or verbal nudge, every participant is a scribe-on-call for logging in notes on an easel sheet at a moment's notice (good news for the hyper). Notes may pertain to highlights of debate, a listing of pros and cons, the tracking of a round robin, or the like. Or they might be brief entries listed and numbered on separate easel sheets pertaining to: ISSUES, TO DO'S, RECOMMENDATIONS, ASSUMPTIONS, CRITICAL SUCCESS FACTORS, GAPS, OVERLAPS, ITEMS FOR NEXT AGENDA, or whatever helps the group's collective brain recall and follow different threads.

This technique is preferable to assigning one person to serve as the group's recording secretary (hear the groans?), because it deals with several realities:

• Much talk is the mud-muck of discovery; there is no rhyme or reason for recording the bulk of it whatsoever, unless some legal matter demands it. Only key points need to be colandered and scrutinized. Also, interruptions by a recording secretary attempting to take nearly verbatim copy can destroy the pace of a meeting, the birth of Ahas!

- Everyone is forced to be a better listener, never knowing when he or she will be called on to enter something on a easel sheet (or on an overhead transparency, which can be revealed periodically if wall space is at a premium). *Note:* To allay the fears of poor spellers, immediately mention that understandable abbreviations or near-correct spellings are okay because getting ideas down quickly is most important. Don't, however, call on scribes who think they're chiseling tombstones.

- Rarely does every person care to speak about the same topic; therefore, draft your scribe-on-call from among those who aren't likely to be advocates at the time (e.g., "Kerry, would you scribe for now, please?"); instant selection becomes easy once you learn to read members.

- Publicly entering notes on easel sheets, believe it or not, can sometimes turn sphinx to kitty cat. Serving the group in this incidental way seems to have the psychological benefit of allowing the contributor to feel *I have worth, I matter to the team and its progress.* You can almost hear the purrs.

- What needs to be recorded is often best logged in *after* there's been an energizing, momentum-building dialogue. The recording becomes a confirming, synthesizing act.

- No one is forced to be pack mule, burdened by producing a *narrative* of minutes distributed too late to be of much help.

Usually, the most helpful minutes from a collaborative meeting consist of one or more of the following, depending on the stage of document-making: copies of selected index cards, transparencies, and the like that were written on during the meeting; copyboard printouts, including reduced facsimiles of easel sheets; and matrices filled in during a meeting or developed from easel-sheet notes afterwards. Following are examples of matrices. Sample A, a consolidation of the matrix headings shown on page 79, is also excellent for stand-up and impromptu get-togethers. Sample B allows "outsiders" to stay in the loop of understanding without becoming JIC-Ps. Sample C, with variations, contains the kind of information a group may need for monitoring a storyboard and contents of a prospective document.

TYPES OF MINUTES

TYPE A

ITEM	ACTION / REASON	DEADLINE
Launching new Angelina line	J. Davis to draft questionnaire to be ready for Focus Group in Memphis	March 18

TYPE B

ISSUE A:	What do we want to learn from the Focus Group session?		
KEY POINTS:	Need to see which age groups are most likely to purchase Winston Products, their three main reasons for wanting to do so, and the possible resistance points. Also need to see if Amato Ltd. poses any significant competition.		
ACTIONS AND DEADLINES:	J. Davis	Draft questionnaire	March 18
	R. Chang	Screen candidates to ensure a demographic cross-section	March 20

Note: Issues B, C, and so on would follow the same pattern.

TYPE C

During our August 21 meeting about the Lansing 40F, we addressed this problem: How might we improve the traffic flow? Below are outcomes.

UNDERLYING PROBLEMS	HOW THEY MIGHT BE CONTROLLED OR ELIMINATED

OR

TENTATIVE CONCLUSIONS	MAJOR SUPPORTING DETAILS

OR

CONCLUSIONS	RECOMMENDATIONS

NELSON: I like seeing a summary of the meeting with action items: Who's doing what? Also, the leader should ask, "Gordon, if you're going to do this, how will you keep the rest of the team informed? Are you going to send the results back to me, disperse them yourself, or what?" We need to communicate with each other about clear deliverables and timing.

Some of the other roles below may or may not be announced ahead of time. You have to decide what is likely to work best in each situation.

Recorder/Publisher. Described more fully in Chapter 15 on group writing, this person staffs a workstation consisting of a personal computer, high-speed laser printer, and, if possible, a desktop copier. Tasks include not only keying in items from easel sheets or debate but also copying members' longhand submissions as needed. The person's primary assignment is piecing together and publishing the group's output document by keeping up with changes on the storyboard as well as integrating and styling the copy produced by team members. By hooking up an LCD panel to the computer, the recorder/publisher might also be called upon to make changes in copy as participants suggest them. With the panel, text is electronically transferred from a computer monitor to a large projection screen.

Surrogate Customer. Though every person should focus on the customer, at times it helps to appoint someone to play the role formally. When appropriate, the designee might say, "As I put on my customer's hat, it would seem to me that. . . ." Also, you might prompt, "Tempest, if you owned $100,000 in triple-A municipals, how might you react to that option?"

Gnat-Swatter. When a couple of techies bore into a subject with all the relish of French chefs debating the best way to channel a mushroom, you'll be delighted to have a participant charged with sighting gnats. All he or she has to do is wave a fly swatter (in eye-dazzling Day-Glo) to make the point and, at the same time, pro-duce chuckles of relief. Gnat-splatting comments include "Perhaps that's a topic you two should take offline" or "I'm afraid we're getting into too much detail [nodding at the clock]; we need to move on." Or you, as facilitator, can interrupt and ask the group, "How many of you are finding this dialogue helpful?" Then, during a serious infestation of the gnats, let deafening silence signal the reply.

Tangent-Spotter. A gnat-swatter might play this role as well because tangents are often caused by participants mired in minutia. They go off on a "bunny trail"—a phrase some tangent-spotters at GTE simply invoke when needed. A spotter might also say, "Hey, guys, we're breaking the first ground rule. Let's get back on track, please." Or, in a less direct way, "I guess I got lost somewhere. I thought we were supposed to be talking about. . . . Did I miss something, or is this an item we should note on TOPICS FOR NEXT AGENDA?" Because many participants are reluctant to cite the detours of colleagues, announcing this position emboldens a delegatee.

WUNDERLIN: Last week I led a meeting of 20. As a last item on the agenda, I put "Topics to Revisit." I also had an easel sheet with that heading. Then, during a meeting, if a topic got to be too detailed or off track, it got put on the easel. Everyone was happy with that because they felt they weren't being shut off. We covered everything and finished right on time. Part of the secret, of course, was that toward the end of the meeting people were eager to leave, so they mentioned only the most important things during the revisit.

Devil's Advocate. When it's important for a participant to play this role, try to speak with the person ahead of time and announce her or his position so others won't think their colleague is an incurable negativist. A devil's advocate giving *constructive* criticism can help prevent group-think, a phenomenon that occurs when people on a closely knit team fail to see blind spots in their decision making. A person highly respected for his or her impartiality can also serve the role in commenting about adversarial positions.

Breakout Captain. At times, you'll anticipate that a breakout group will have to handle a task related to an upcoming agenda item—a common occurrence when participants share writing assignments. Before the exchange begins, you might ask or appoint a volunteer to captain the breakout. (E.g., "Jim, I see the air-fuel mixture is a key topic on the storyboard. Since you're the major stakeholder in that area, would you please head the breakout on it? What we're going to talk about next may provide you with some essential information.") The volunteer is likely to listen better and not panic or ask for a revisit when the rubber hits the road. If pacing permits, you might appoint the entire subgroup before proceeding.

Recapper. To encourage all participants to prick up their ears, especially during a teleconference, periodically call on someone to summarize. Once in a while it helps if the same person performs the task throughout a meeting. Most frequently, however, the element of surprise works to a group's advantage.

> "I can tell more about how a company's doing by asking everyone if they're having fun than I can by poring over financial statements. . . . [In my own company] I always ask the chief financial officer if he's having fun, too. After all, my mama didn't raise a fool."
>
> *Bill Fromm*
> *President, Barkley & Green*
> *Advertising*

Spiker. This person need only hold up a seven-inch aluminum gutter nail, signaling, "Let's spike it! Let's end the debate. We're repeating ourselves." As with the fly swatter, the act usually evokes ripples of laughter punctuated by a huge, collective sigh. After agreeing on a point or after a give-and-take has drawn to its natural conclusion, people tend to talk beyond it—perhaps for reassurance—and unless you or the spiker intervenes, fat gathers fast.

Nails holding rain gutters along eaves of roofs aren't necessary, of course. But I have found that, in the spirit of fun and play critical to many a collaborative get-together, distributing nails to participants as they near decision making encourages each to become a spiker. It's especially effective when a person near an overhead projector flicks it on to "blow up" a spike the size of Mount Rushmore. WOW! Does that help momentum big time!

ASSIGNING TASKS

Having fun makes doling out assignments a lot easier. Besides, if you tend to such issues with the suggestions given on pages 77–80, delegating tasks will pose few, if any, problems, except, perhaps, for an occasional cabbage. But even then, there's always hope. For when people are—to use a couple of well-earned clichés—inspired by a visionary leader and fired with enthusiasm, the fundamental truth still holds firm: the human spirit has no bounds.

part III

BOUILLABAISSE:

"As with many traditional French dishes, its precise list of ingredients is a matter of often heated controversy, with different parties insisting on their own particular selection of fish . . . The word *bouillabaisse* is a French version of Provencal *bouiabaisso*, literally 'boil and settle'—supposedly what the cook says to the cooking pot."

The Diner's Dictionary

better than a fortune cookie

Enticing the reluctant with a benefit-driven meeting announcement

The ""firefighters"" in business sprint from meeting to meeting. They're the great panters and ranters in office corridors. A meeting announcement from one of them—if you're lucky—is hardly longer than a tittle of a note in a fortune cookie:

> *There'll be a meeting of the Sigma Task Force in Room A on Monday, April 3, beginning at 9. Please plan to attend.*

Or perhaps you'll get a tad more:

> *At 10:00 tomorrow there will be a meeting of the Q-Team in 17E to discuss the Morganville proposal. Call Debby to confirm.*

Would you know how or what to prepare for with either meeting? Of course not! But haven't we all been noosed by such notices? Their sketchiness is a major cause of group grope, in which baffled and irritated participants share

112

thoughts similar to those that follow. They were expressed during a meeting audit conducted for a vice president of information management and his reports—both direct and dotted line:

- *Floyd thinks an announcement with agenda will mean too much structure. But it's structure that gets things done and gives a group momentum.*

- *All he does is throw tea leaves on the water and asks us to read them. It's a farce. I can't prepare much at all, and that's why I get angry.*

- *He thinks because "Tuesday morning" is a routine thing, everyone knows what the agenda is. So here's what happens: individuals bring their pet concerns to a flea market of a meeting, each hoping for a buy-in that deals with the symptoms of an issue. What happens, of course, is that deep-seated causes rarely get addressed.*

Imagine the mayhem when the dotted-line people reported back to Floyd's counterparts, trying to recapture the seltzer bubbles of talk. The old game of "Gossip" grew big time! So did the turmoil.

HELPMATE FOR BOTH CALLER AND CALLED

The basic meeting announcement is a variation on the prompts of the All-Purpose Request (Chapter 5). It essentially says I REQUEST you to come to this particular meeting to help achieve the BENEFIT(S) cited. We'll derive the benefits by completing the verb-spurred ACTION PLAN (i.e., agenda) shown with TIME ON TASK for each item.

The announcement may also give BACKGROUND that puts the meeting into context, or request that prospective participants complete certain tasks for which the group need not meet to discuss. On occasions a note may scope out what will *not* be covered in the meeting—and why—to avert any RESULT OF DELAY (see the prompt in the All Purpose Request) that might lie in addressing an irrelevant or premature topic.

LA ROSA: Here we live or die by an online scheduler. When I first came here, I was appalled because people could schedule my day away, and I *still* feel that way. It's wonderful to get everybody on the same page, but other departments [over which I have no control] tend to book as many meetings as they want. It's something we're trying hard to work on.

A SAMPLE ANNOUNCEMENT

Meeting leaders who *really* get things done are seldom seen flapping about. Why? Because they take time to plan their major get-togethers, including an announcement sent to prospective participants within 24 to 48 hours of a gathering. For example:

DATE: March 29, 19—

TO: Denise Benedetti   Ross Jackson (Sigma Liaison)
Bill Casco (Scribe)   J.P. Levinger
Leanna Harmon   Sally Ramirez (Finance Dept.)

FR: Karen Winslow-Rogers—Ext. 9827

RE: MEETING OF THE SIGMA TASK FORCE
MONDAY, APRIL 3
10:30–11:45
CONFERENCE ROOM A, 4TH FLOOR
ESTIMATED COST: $1200

BENEFIT(S): Tim O'Malley, lead engineer at Sigma, will be here to update his specifications and to give us a chance to adjust due dates on delivery of parts.

BACKGROUND: Sigma's design has been affected by recent emission constraints passed by the state legislature. The completed job represents $3.5M in revenue.

PREP ALERT: Before the meeting please:

Outline (and bring to the meeting) one overhead transparency of a schedule you could meet, allowing for logistics and holidays.

AGENDA: At the meeting we will:

10:30   Question Tim about the specs, particularly in regard to his concerns about quality control.
11:00   Recap and assign tasks for the preceding item.
11:10   Consolidate your individually preferred due dates into a master calendar.
11:20   Get Tim's buy-in of the schedule.
11:35   List possible items for the May agenda.
11:45   Adjourn

SCOPE NOTE: To ensure the meeting stays on track, we'll defer critiques of the latex formulation until R&D finishes its investigation.

The Prompts—With Annotations

Under a microscope, the parts of the sample announcement reveal many significant, fat-scrapping advantages, as described below. Once you internalize the parts, you can adapt the format for just about any kind of meeting—even one only hours away. Also, heed the advice whether you issue an announcement on paper or on screen.

REQUEST (implied by the prompts TO, FR, and RE)

To: **Cite the participants, sometimes indicating roles, titles, or the like:**

Charlotte Higgins (Scribe)
Carlton Wu (Tek-Neeto, Inc.)

Such a listing helps convey the importance of the meeting, what the dynamics are likely to be, the levels of knowledge and interest to be considered for presentations, and so on.

Check the list against the agenda (action items) to make sure you haven't overlooked someone who should attend. In meetings without an agenda, it's not uncommon to discover certain people were needed but are "now unavailable." And even if the meeting slops along without them, the items are likely to be revisited when the people finally appear. That's fat!

Exclude those who do not need to attend. Most will appreciate your gesture, except perhaps for one or two who will ask, "Why wasn't I invited?" Referring them to the benefits and agenda helps when you reply, "I didn't want to steal your time for something that seemed unrelated to your work. Did I err in that regard?"

FR: **Give title or position, when appropriate, as well as a phone number, e-mail address, or the like.**

RE: **Make sure you give the meeting the what-where-and-when test. Highlight the copy so it stands out as a reminder if needed to be glimpsed again.**

Do not call an initial get-together hoping every person will come. It's extremely difficult to find a date accommodating everyone's frantic pace. Instead, try to corral as many people as possible by quickly polling them ahead of time about their availability. In your survey, emphasize how they will benefit from the meeting: "To make sure you get into the loop early . . . or hear about ways to cut weeks off your project." Avoid immediate, egocentric turn-offs, such as "I need to . . . " "I'm thinking about calling . . ." or the like.

Cite the intended length of the meeting after you write a verb-spurred agenda (as described in the next chapter). A verb reveals a procedure (*list, recap, consolidate*) and hints at the time needed to complete it.

Estimate the cost of the meeting by considering salary levels as well as overhead. Remind people that time is money. Say to them in subtle ways: *Come prepared. I'm doing that, as you can see by my announcement.*

BENEFIT(S). Call it PURPOSE if you wish, but be sure to tell the participants how they—and implicitly, the customer—will benefit from the meeting. Answer these questions: *Why should I come? What am I going to get out of it? How will it help our business?* When such questions go unanswered—as they generally do—"excuses" flourish:

- *Sorry, Craig, I'm going to be out of town.*
- *That's not a good date for me, Jordan.*
- *I wish I could be there, Shirl, but I have a conflict.*

Translation: *I prefer doing something else—perhaps even going to a different meeting—that offers clearer and more compelling benefits.*

Benefit statements are superb cost-choppers. They help you sort the critical from the trivial, the must dos from the nice-to-dos that suck the unwary into the activity trap. Wrestling with a benefit statement forces you to test old habits or to gain insights you might not otherwise discover. For example:

- Hmm . . . perhaps I shouldn't be holding this kind of meeting. It has simply become institutionalized over the years, a vestige from the days of Old Man McLenahan. Its original intent no longer exists.

- For this meeting I don't need Althea, Dion, or Billie Marie, but I had better include Marjorie Kovacs from R&D. She's the expert on polymers.

If you're a Wing-It who calls meetings on the fly, coming up with a benefit statement to appeal to prospective attendees will demand discipline and new behavior. At first, because of a frenzied approach to things, you won't want to take time. You'll be tempted to shoot your arms skyward and bark, "I can't think of a benefit . . . they've just gotta do it!" But beware: The gottas can getcha! Unquestioning them can hobble you with inefficiencies, fat, and failure.

BACKGROUND. Give background only when you need to provide context to a meeting—usually a first-time get-together or an issue-oriented powwow. When people understand *the part* (this particular meeting) in relationship to *the whole* (the business driver behind the meeting), they are more likely to become engaged in the event. If, however, participants come to a meeting puzzled or confused, simmerings of displeasure will bubble up as negativism, sarcasm, indecision.

Background can also help eliminate queries at the beginning of a meeting. If one is called for no apparent reason, a person may attempt to probe the *why* of the *what* and inadvertently open a floodgate of unnecessary discussion.

PREP ALERT. Save still more time in the meeting by having participants complete selected tasks beforehand. But make sure they aren't overwhelming or devoid of any obvious connection to the benefits and the agenda. Tasks aimed at streamlining an upcoming meeting might include:

- brainstorming ideas to be submitted and combined with those of other participants, thus providing a common springboard for the get-together
- annotating a draft in response to a specific set of questions
- reading certain materials, while also noting the meeting will be run on the assumption they've been studied

Be sure participants understand what steps to take, by using this lead-in: *Before the meeting, please. . . .* In fact, if you create a template for the announcement, make the phrase part of it. Then complete the sentence, starting with a precise verb for each entry.

Also view this part of the announcement as an opportunity to involve those who seem reticent during a meeting but, unlike their more vocal colleagues, simply prefer to reflect and ruminate in private.

AGENDA. Realize a verb-spurred agenda, shown in the next chapter, is really an ACTION PLAN driven by the BENEFITS. The two must dovetail. With satisfactory completion of the action plan (i.e., the agenda), benefits are achieved. *Note:* At times you may want to make the agenda a separate document, especially when annotated entries might be helpful. In that case, simply refer readers to a subsequent screen or attached page.

Make sure each entry of the action plan is verb-driven by using this lead-in: *At the meeting we will. . . .* A main verb must follow the helping verb.

SCOPE NOTE. Indicate what will not be covered in the meeting and why. It helps everyone's focus. Furthermore, framing the meeting discourages JIC-Ps and who knows what other interloping, group-groping fat-feeders!

KNOSKA: When I go to a meeting where somebody says we're going to meet from 7:30 till 9 or 10, I shudder. Why? Because for me that time from 9 to 10 is wasted time. The caller is not sure the meeting will go beyond 9, so I can't schedule anything or do what I want to do because of their inability to plan well.

---

10 barred: picnics at the peak of gnat season

Avoiding chaos with results-targeted agendas

A meeting without an agenda is a call to chaos. It's a picnic at the peak of gnat season, lotto fever at the 7-Eleven, a rock concert where Hootie & the Blowfish are no-shows. Yet people, especially those among the Hit-and-Run Set, persist in calling such powwows and then wonder why they feel enervated rather than energized, forgetting they have about as much chance of success with them as they would trying to stem the silt flows at the mouth of the Mississippi.

An agenda is key to planning meetings. Without one, the caller of a meeting often:

- appears unprepared, unprofessional, and vulnerable to anyone tempted to wrest control

  Result: Type A's in the group take over—or depart! The convener's reputation becomes chopped meat in the rumor mill and charbroiled in any "360" appraisal program.

- runs his or her group amok, often to the brink of mutiny

  Result: Frustrated members manifest their feelings in anger and antagonism, curtness, passive-aggressive silences, complaints, incomplete assignments, and so on.

- continues to rehash items meeting after meeting after meeting

  Result: Absentees multiply, as do the come-and-goers. Yakaphiliacs, tangent-drifters, and gnat-sifters, all of whom feed on the fodder of rehashings, contribute to the cycle as well.

- increases the number of so-called "emergency meetings," which spring from earlier gatherings where objectives were unclear, the course was foggy, and closure was either ambiguous or nonexistent

  Result: Productivity drops, as it also does in the previous cases.

- spends countless hours trying to counter rumors, accusations of turf invasion, and all kinds of *mis*communication

  Result: Productivity plunges, customers get lost in the shuffle, and the person's career finally plateaus or ends.

NO AGENDA? HEAR WHAT *YOU* ARE SAYING

In their more than 50 years of research on nonverbal communication, Edward T. Hall and Mildred Reed Hall, the renowned anthropologists and authorities on international business relationships, have drawn this conclusion:

> Some 80 to 90 percent of the significant features of a culture are reflected in its nonverbal messages. These are usually taken for granted and transmitted unconsciously. Nonverbal messages are highly situational in character. Furthermore, the meanings of such messages are unique to each culture and often charged with emotion.

In this country, meeting without an agenda delivers powerful nonverbal messages—messages you may need to hear *loudly and clearly* if you simply prefer "calling the gang together" because you think, "I can handle it." Here are possible messages sent by such conveners, whose lack of an agenda puts more fat on the flank of meetings than perhaps any other act:

- I don't care about productivity and customers. If I did, I wouldn't be here plucking hairs from a caterpillar.

- I'm really a wimp masquerading as either a "pal who likes rap sessions" or a "libido-driven piledriver." Underneath the mask, I'm scared to death, for I haven't the foggiest idea of what I really want to accomplish. Help me, but pretend you don't see through me.

- I see no connection between what company officials are trying to achieve in the way of cultural change and the way I conduct my meetings. All that talk about "the best leaders are visionaries and motivators" is horsefeathers! I've gotten away with my gig for ages. The Peter Principle is alive and well.

THE VERB-SPURRED AGENDA: KEY TO THE 3 P'S

What millions of meeting conveners need to work with is a verb-spurred agenda. It's the key to preparation, participation, and progress. Unlike a *topical* agenda, which is rarely worth the screen or paper it's written on, a *verb-spurred* agenda provides focus, a beacon for the leader as much as for the participants. Note the contrast:

Topical Agenda

1. FS and FC Tables
2. Cycle 33
3. Testing

Verb-Spurred Agenda

10:00 *Examine* need to build FS and FC Tables
10:25 *Recap* and *assign* tasks
10:35 *List* problems with Cycle 33
10:50 *Approve* steps for October test
11:10 *Recap* and *assign* tasks

An entry in a topical agenda hints only at the *what,* which leaves the matter hazy and eventually subject to sabotage—deliberate or otherwise. What's more, topical agendas usually consist of nouns and adjectives just plopped on the page or screen, beached whales to be contended with somehow. Active verbs, however, connote precision, momentum, progress. They help organize and energize.

A Topical Agenda Often Dooms a Meeting!

The topical agenda can also become a participant's source of irritation as she or he tries to prepare for a meeting. Jennifer and Myron, who have no idea what's going to happen, labor a day or so to cover every possible contingency. Lyle guesses, but during the meeting discovers he didn't guess right. Carl, Eunice, and Zhen just don't worry about it; they prefer to sit in silence rather than spend hours preparing for something they can't be sure of. And after years of experience, the old warhorses shrug and ignore the agenda altogether—simply another fly to flit. Yet the topical agenda deludes its users into thinking, "I know how to run a meeting," when, in fact, the topical agenda—just like no agenda at all—often dooms a get-together from the pop of the starter's pistol.

Increasing Your Chances for Success

In a verb-driven agenda, the entry tells the *how* (via the verb) and the *what* (via the object). It's the action plan driven by the potential benefits. *It's the device that controls the process and thereby controls the participants.* It's a key to providing and maintaining momentum. In the end it's a measure against which to judge progress. What's more, each specific verb, as shown below, gives clues to the procedures, the kinds of materials, and the time allotments needed for dealing with an entry:

> *Draft* entries for the October test.
> *Approve* steps for the October test.
> *Outline* steps for the October test.

Verb-driven entries can also indicate the substeps of a process, thus helping a group master both clock and Parkinson's Law.

Item B: Determine Potential Synergy

2:30–2:35	Identify category of need
2:35–2:45	Hear background
2:45–3:00	Clarify understandings
3:00–3:20	Estimate costs

METZGER: A major problem occurs when a group gets together [for a teleconference] and there's no leader, no agenda. I can hardly keep from jumping in, but the professional protocols of our service prevent that.

HOWELL: I don't like meetings that run on. Any topic that comes to the table has to benefit the common conversation.

Kill *Discuss* and *Review*

Two verbs to avoid like garlic in a strawberry sundae are *discuss* and *review*. Not only are they worthless, but they make entries subject to diversions and prolonged discourse—a menu gone amok.

Discussion underlies every meeting, whether the give-and-take is held to *understand*, to *compare*, to *decide*, or whatever. *Review*, on the other hand, too often means *let's rehash or procrastinate*. More specific, results-oriented verbs are shown in the box on page 123. Use them wisely and precisely.

Recap as You Go Along

As you plan your agenda, let the verbs reveal which items will demand summarization and follow-up during the meeting. Then insert the "recap lines" on the agenda (see page 120) to foster the necessary discipline. Otherwise, you'll find yourself bellowing out assignments as the Type A's stampede the door.

Working It to the Max!

To exploit an agenda fully, consider these other tips as well:

- Distribute the agenda ahead of time. If that's not possible, then jot the agenda down on a chalkboard, easel sheet, copyboard, or the like just before the hastily convened meeting begins.

- Limit the number of items—perhaps three to five—for an hour-long meeting. Focus on the critical, not the trivial; the more closely related the items, the better.

- Focus on what the group is striving toward instead of lingering in the past.

VERBS TO SPUR YOUR AGENDAS

add	debate	judge	report
agree on	decide	jump-start	resolve
assign	delegate	list	rewrite
audit	delete	listen to	revise
brainstorm	deliver	make	round-robin
build	determine	map	schedule
calculate	divide	negotiate	select
check	draft	organize	set up
classify	edit	persuade	share
combine	evaluate	plan	simplify
compare	explain	prepare	sketch
compile	find	present	solve
complete	force-rank	preview	suggest
compute	gather	rank	summarize
conduct	give	rate	tell
confirm	hear	read	trace
continue	illustrate	recommend	write

- Phrase things positively, emphasizing opportunities. Rather than say, At the meeting we will . . . *evaluate the Gazette's recent criticism of Dullstat, Inc.*, distribute copies of the article or assume the news has already spread. Then consider an entry like this: *brainstorm ways to help Dullstat become known as a highly respected corporate citizen.*

KNOSKA: If you have a multifaceted agenda calling for a multitude of decisions, you're not going to make many that are good.

- Post a copy of the agenda in the room, enlarged if necessary, for all to see without binoculars. As each item is completed, cross it off to signify the

WHATEVER-MEANING-YOU-LIKE VERBS

Be suspicious of overused words that have lost their precision in business. If you favor any of the following, make sure meanings are clear.

administer	coordinate	examine	investigate
analyze	develop	expedite	manage
assure	ensure	follow up	observe
collaborate	establish	implement	perform

group's progress. *Note:* You may also want to consider putting an agenda on a transparency and then displaying it from one of two overhead projectors, while the other is free for sketching and presenting. Or if you're working with a computer and an LCD panel, project the agenda each time an item has been accomplished, including all the motivating strike-thru's.

- Organize the topics in a logical flow so participants can make smooth transitions in their thinking. Too often an agenda of disparate items is equivalent to demanding that participants leadfoot the accelerator, shift to reverse, turn on the wipers, paw into the glove compartment, and slam on the brakes—all within seconds of each other.

- Plan breaks to allow for significant gear shifts and to give the more "reflective types" time to digest the give-and-take before feeling comfortable enough to share their viewpoints.

DELMONT: One of the biggest violations of meetings is that people never come back on time from breaks. They drift in because they were trying to find a phone or whatever. So schedule two half-hour breaks during a full-day session and a couple of stretch breaks. For our quarterly sales meetings, we set up a communication room next to our meeting room in the hotel. In it are cell phones, fax machines, and an attendant. It's a big time-saver that keeps a meeting on schedule.

- Start and end with items that are brief and easy to handle and that have a positive impact. This technique also permits the occasional latecomer to take part in a more substantive second item on the agenda without missing pertinent facts.

- Consider balancing a plain-vanilla topic with one that's five-alarm chili. Or think about running the rapids after canoeing a couple of streams, or orchestrating quartets, duets, and recitatives in a cantata. Decide what will work well, when, why, and for whom.

- Include the more controversial items near the beginning of a meeting, when energy levels tend to be higher and attention spans longer.

- Think about presenters. When could they serve the meeting best while minimizing interruptions to their work flow?

- Three-hole punch hard copies of agendas and encourage members to keep them in binders you've labeled with the committee name as well as the startup date and, whenever appropriate, the intended sunset. Distribute the binders at the first or second meeting, a symbolic act that says, *We're going to set sail, make progress, and reach our destination with your help at the helm; we're in this together.* Suggest that agendas, handouts, and related minutes and materials be kept as a chronological refresher and incubator for the members, a quick update for any alternate, or both.

A Dynamic, Fluid One

When people collaborate more than report, a meeting (or a series of related meetings) becomes a process of discovery, of creating a shared understanding. Enroute to the collective insight, the original agenda must be viewed flexibly while participants remain on track. To accommodate the process, members may have to stop periodically and alter the meeting's "flight plan"—sometimes slightly, sometimes significantly. In either case, precise verbs speed the changes when the following lead-in is written on an easel sheet, transparency, or computer screen: *For the next segment we need to. . . .* Suggested entries are then either elicited from the group or, faster yet, outlined by a small subgroup during a brief stretch break.

Without seeing and agreeing on agenda adjustments, many collaborative bodies find time allotments get ignored, discourse blurs, and the turbulence of group grope undermines the mission. With well-oiled teams, however, the agenda often becomes intuitive and fluid, not always demanding a formal readjustment. To onlookers, the group activity might seem informal, but it's steeled by shared, collaborative underpinnings.

AN ISSUE-FOCUSED AGENDA

In addition to the verb-driven agenda, there's another important type, one that features only an issue or two. An entry might appear as follows, with the issue shown in boldface or all caps and, when helpful, annotated:

Agenda

10:00–10:30 How might we make up for a potential three-week delay if we go with Balen?

Adapting the Darco agreement has worked well in the past, but Balen Associates has links to a number of our direct competitors. Our legal department might want to draft something completely new, which could delay the project launch by three weeks at least. Please reread the Darco agreement and be ready to offer your suggestions.

10:30–10:40 Break

In a topical agenda, such an issue might simply be reduced to:

Non-disclosure with Balen Associates

The entry, if not framed and explained by the convener during the meeting, would succumb to scatterbrained thinking. Each member of the group would bring her or his own preconceptions about the topic.

In a verb-spurred agenda, however, the entry might appear like this:

Determine ways to avoid Balen contract delays

Participants, informed further by an annotation, would be able to prepare fairly well. In fact, the outcome might be the same as with an issue-focused agenda, in which a convener looks at an issue through the filter of a complete question. The construct is an absolute must for this type of meeting map. A complete question guides not only the group's common perception of an issue and its underlying assumptions but also the course of resolution. "A problem well stated," said Charles Kettering, "is a problem half solved." What's more, a complete question determines the type and length of deliberation likely to be engendered. Consider, for example, how each of the following questions would affect discourse and its duration:

- *Could using the Darco nondisclosure agreement save time with Balen Associates?*
- *What risks, if any, are there in adapting Darco's nondisclosure for the Balen deal?*
- *Any problems with Darco vis á vis Balen?*
- *How should we handle Balen?*
- *What do you think of Paragraph 7.5 in the proposed Balen agreement?*

When you know or sense an issue's at stake, try this kind of agenda as the basis for effective debate. Scrutinize the wording of each question you draft. Then decide on the one that will frame the give-and-take fairly and accurately.

PEEPLES: I start with the basic: "Why are we having this meeting?" Then I ask: "What are the participants going to leave with? Are they going to leave with assignments, understandings, or the task of going out and coming back with questions, issues related to a problem, or what?" I must consider the take-away.

Annotations

Annotating an issue, or even a first-time entry on a verb-spurred agenda, can also serve to remind participants of key facts, educate them about new ones, or diminish endless, fat-inducing ruminations during a meeting.

Composing the notes will, of course, take a few minutes. But the tradeoff in communicating an understanding clearly and concisely will be not having to waste hours in emergency runs while the heart of the organization—the meetings on which it thrives—continues to clot and convulse.

11

endless
corkscrews

*Following step-by-step procedure
maps to guide the give-and-take of
collaborative journeys*

"What do we do *now*?" That's the baffler committee members wrestle with when they have no agenda, or a typical topical compilation, or an agenda relying on *discuss* and *review*. Twisting and turning, their meeting becomes an endless corkscrew.

A verb-spurred agenda prevents that. The specific action verbs give clues to the procedure maps that set direction, scrap the fat of chitchat, and speed progress. A procedure map outlines the steps that comprise a major activity, such as brainstorming, problemsolving, and the like. The following is one example of how a map might be developed, starting with this entry:

Evaluate feedback from the attitude survey

An effective meeting leader will look at the entry and quickly think: *What steps might help in processing the evaluation?* In answer, the person might key in or jot down the following procedure:

1. Study overhead graphic of major results.
2. Round-robin each person's first impression.
3. Distribute and explain handout of statistics.
4. Break into small groups for specific survey categories.
5. Comment on each group's overhead foil re: recommendations.

Then, examining the potential map, the leader might further anticipate and estimate:

• Do any of the steps call for handouts, breakout assignments, breakout rooms, or special items? If so, how will they be tended to, and when?
• About how much time will these steps take?
• Is there any way to make them leaner?
• Do the steps look as if they will move things along, not allowing the group to run into potholes, detours, or dead ends? If not, what are the alternatives?

Answers might reveal the need for a more valuable or compelling task (e.g., *Recommend company initiatives from results of attitude survey*) that demands an altogether different procedure map. Or the original entry (*Evaluate feedback from the attitude survey*) might seem fine except for the need to tweak one or more of the five steps shown above. Eventually the map might be turned into a transparency, handout, or easel sheet for committee members to be shown at the appropriate point:

Here's how we might tackle the next agenda item. Would these steps help?

OR

For this item we could follow these steps. Do they seem reasonable? [PAUSE] *Any changes?*

Although participants should be given an opportunity to replace or alter the steps if they wish, my experience indicates wholesale changes are rare. Sometimes the entry might be supplanted by another pressing matter, and the transparency—the format I prefer—is saved in my Facilitator's Handbook for another occasion. At other times, a committee member might suggest a minor change to a procedure.

Invariably, however, groups appreciate the forethought, the time gained by having a map to follow, and the feeling that there's a firm but steady hand at the helm. They would, of course, resent and resist coercion, but they do find comfort in a leader who guides them where they believe they need to go.

CAMERON: Sitting at a console right next to the flight director is one of the astronauts from a previous mission. Before our mission, we train with them on integrated simulation. They know me [the commander], the rest of the crew, and when the sticky parts of the mission are. They've got their procedures open. They know what we're doing and what we're supposed to be doing. They can really make your day—or save you in some cases. So when they call, I listen.

Now if any of you readers firefight quick fixes and are about to howl, "I don't have time for all that stuff," hold your hoses! Relax for a minute. Consider the advantages of having procedure maps, 20 percent of which—after you've created them—can be used 80 percent of the time for other meetings.

- Without procedures, meeting members criss-cross rocks and rills like lost sheep, furious at the lack of direction, which is all the more reason to sketch a map quickly in response to a legitimate 9-1-1. Step-by-step sequences also help keep videoconferences, and especially teleconferences, from leading sheep into brambles.

- Helping a group agree on "next steps" during an involved or controversial meeting, which has to be done occasionally, can turn into hours of haggling if a jellyfish leader, with no sense for "process," loses control.

- Whatever time it takes to generate a map—before or during a meeting—is often minuscule compared to the hours devoured by such things as clockless rooms, delayed startups, excessive socializing, and the myriad attempts at getting somewhere, only to be frustrated by characters allowed to ego-trip, race, grumble, or—brace yourself!—dissect a topic as if they were eating hominy grits with toothpicks.

In short, it takes time to save time. By controlling the process, you control the participants. So hang up your hoses, you firefighters, and get down to work—truly *productive* work—because the efficiencies of "processing," not to mention the positive effects on esprit de corps, will make you mapping mavens.

MAP-SCRAPPING THE FAT

To start compiling sets of procedures, consider the samples below. They deal with the six maps from which groups can most commonly benefit.

Map A: Problemsolving

Note: Boldface type indicates what might be shown as a procedure map on a transparency. The annotations for your understanding can, of course, be shared orally with team members or adapted on handouts of the maps. Also, realize that not all steps need to be completed in a single get-together; at times it may be helpful to adjourn and let people reflect and gain critical distance from an issue before continuing.

1. **Verbalize observations.** Have each participant state her or his perception of the problem in terms of things seen or heard. Involve all members in round-robin feedback, after giving the introverts, in particular, a bit of time to reflect or make notes on their 3 × 5s.

2. **Agree on and write down the problem as a complete question.** Often the beginning words and the operative verb in a complete question help create a shared perception of a problem, as noted with the Darco/Balen contrast on page 127. The wording also affects the direction of the solution. For example:

   • *How can we reduce overtime?* (Potential solutions center on how "we" will do it. The wording might also limit some people's thinking to a solitary idea.)

   • *What are ways to reduce overtime?* (Potential solutions and their sources aren't limited.)

   • *What can be done to prevent overtime?* (Prevention = total reduction.)

   Also, be careful of the word *and* in a question, such as, "How can we improve the speed *and* accuracy of Dyna-Syst?" There, two questions have been combined, but the solutions for each may or may not be mutually exclusive. Besides, minds trying to track two or more significant threads at once contribute to muddled meetings and assailable decisions.

3. **Analyze it.** Break down the problem to see how various forces contribute to it. Asking "Five Whys"—a technique favored at General Tire—can be a whopper of a chopper here, or sometimes a substitute for steps 1 to 3 altogether. For example: *Why so many returns? (Because customers didn't like the product.) Why? (They didn't like the design.) Why? (It was clumsy.) Why? (The handle was too small.) Why? (An error in the formulation caused the plastic to shrink.)*

4. **Brainstorm possible solutions.** See Map D below.

5. **Agree on criteria for evaluation.** Stop! Halt! Don't budge another inch until criteria have been established. Interminable talk, half-baked solutions, or both often arise by ignoring or overlooking this critical step.

6. **Rank the solutions.** Discover which solutions have greatest appeal. Don't spend time on barrel bottoms unless gleaning an element to enhance a top-ranked alternative.

7. **Round-robin and record the pros and cons.** Explore *advantages* first—a must, to avoid premature, time-eroding haggling—and then *disadvantages* of the top-ranked solutions, urging everyone to give feedback. List and number key comments for public viewing and to tick-mark shared sentiments. In many cases, watch the marks gradually reveal clusters of agreement that may either narrow the debate or accelerate consensus. (Also see "Assess the Options," page 38.)

8. **Make a decision.** See Map F below.

WALTON: As a leader, I have to believe the process will work. Then I must choose structures that others can see. When they begin to believe it, too, then they can see it. My confidence must make it carry. I also recommend that when a decision has been made, the results should be confirmed several times. Make sure everyone's in agreement. Then take the decision to the next highest level as soon as possible. Speed impresses people. It also discourages second-guessing.

Map B: Wording a Definition or Problem Statement

One of the worst glob-hobblers for a committee is to spend time on wording a definition, problem statement, or the like that's central to deliberation, progress, and the clarity of a final report. Days can go down the drain because of disagreements over nuances. And for some inexplicable, though perhaps Satanic, reason, at least one committee member invariably grinds away at the copy like an inchworm faceting diamonds. The following procedure accommodates the worm while relieving those who couldn't care a whit.

1. **Write a draft with lines numbered on the left.** Invite any member impassioned about a definition or problem statement to write his or her copy on a transparency, consecutively numbering lines at the left. Typically, I find only a very small percentage of people are rabid Websters—the few who would churn up the group if this procedure map were not followed.

2. **Preview each draft.** Read each draft without anyone in the group commenting.

3. **Select the preferred draft.** Ask members, by show of hands or numbers on index cards they hold up, to indicate which draft seems "most workable," the one that comes closest to reflecting the meaning that should be commonly understood during deliberations.

4. **Make suggestions for major areas of improvement.** On the transparency of the selected draft, jot notes of suggestions made by group members. Notes should pertain mainly to content, i.e., omitted concepts, ambiguities, need for restrictive phrases, and so on. Encourage respondents to cite line numbers for the group's quick reference. If helpful, indicate parts of the other drafts that might be considered during revision.

5. **Take a break while a subgroup revises a final draft.** Ask for volunteers to meet in a small breakout group and, with the annotated draft, come up with a revised version on a new transparency. Appoint someone to chair the group, preferably anyone but the worm.

Note: This step can usually be executed in 15 minutes or so when the breakout group feels the pressure of awaiting teammates, a situation Mr. Parkinson would've applauded. In a day-long session, you might ask the breakout group to meet during an extended lunch period if other A.M. agenda items can be handled without immediate agreement on revised text. The step offers both the impassioned few and perhaps a quiet one or two a chance to deal with an issue they care about. Failure to respect and acknowledge their needs can easily backfire.

6. **Reconvene to approve and proceed.** Allow for justifiable wordsmithing, requiring the worm and others to explain the *why* of any *what.*

Map C: Testing Assumptions for Problemfinding

1. **State the likely problem as a complete question.** Invite each group member to write down—at the top of a transparency—the question best stating his or her perception of the problem. For example: *How can we eliminate scrap?*

2. **Number and list the underlying assumptions to the question.**

   a. Having scrap is not good.

   b. No scrap at all is ideal.

   c. There must be a way to eliminate it.

   d. There's a problem somewhere in manufacturing.

   e. Manufacturing may or may not be concerned about the scrap.

3. **Project and collect.** Have each person display her or his transparency and add assumptions colleagues contribute.

4. **Debate and discover.** Debate the assumptions to make discoveries and reach consensus about the source of the *real* problem—and its ultimate solution.

NELSON: I find people often "fill in gaps that aren't there." When you say something, it triggers something totally different in the listeners from what *you're* thinking about. That's the constant enemy each of us has to fight. We have to get people to understand what their backgrounds of understandings are and then bring them to a point where they need to be.

Map D: Brainstorming

Groupware is especially good for brainstorming if participants are equally adept at keyboard skills.

1. **State the issue.** Agree on the issue, preferably stated in a question beginning with *how* or *why*:
   - *How can traffic congestion on Secunda Parkway be alleviated during commuting hours?*
   - *Why is traffic on Secunda Parkway increasing during commuting hours?*

2. **Set a stretch quota.** Designate an outlandish number of ideas to stockpile—perhaps 150 for a group of seven or so—to shove people beyond the obvious, to get them into the realm of the silly and ridiculous, where the best ideas tend to nest.

3. **Brainstorm individually.** Have each participant, as fast as possible, list mind-busters on an index card or piece of paper. Also consider one idea per Post-it, written in large letters to expedite feedback.

4. **Round-robin the feedback.** Go around the room, asking each participant to cite one thought at a time as the ideas are recorded on an easel sheet, copyboard, or the like. If Post-its have been used, ask participants to stick their responses on a wall.

5. **Piggyback ideas and force-rank them, if helpful.** Let the accumulated responses trigger other ideas to achieve or surpass the stretch quota. Then, if helpful, force-rank the items (see below), depending on the group's objectives and criteria for evaluation.

Map E: Force-Ranking Ten or More Items

This is a fast and an almost amazing way to discover where preferences center around certain alternatives, the most important criteria, the most appealing ideas in a brainstorm list, or similar choices. It's a technique a General Electric manager taught me years ago. Though I can't remember the person's name, she has saved me—and groups I've worked with—hundreds and hundreds of hours. For we've all curled toes to heels while hearing one person after another ticking favorites: "I'd like to put a tick mark on Number 2 . . . and hmm, let's see, Number 12 . . . and wait-a-minute-go-back-to-Number-7-and-tick-that, and. . . ." Who gives a hoot?

TO WHIP UP A BRAINSTORM

1. Toss a Koosh ball—like a hot potato—from one person to another; each person must instantly blurt out an idea when he or she catches the ball.

2. Hand out, at random, one card from a deck of cards for each suggestion made. Give a prize to the "winner" who has the highest total, with an ace equaling 20 points.

3. Clip and distribute sets of Yellow Pages or pages from mail-order catalogs to spur "connection-making."

The procedure may have to be used twice when a list of items is very long, the second time limited to the top-ranked survivors of the first round.

1. **List and letter the choices.** Usually the options have come from brainstorming, deliberation, or both. Lettering prevents confusion later, e.g., "I give three points to B" vs. "I give three points to 2."

2. **Assume you have ten points to distribute.** Distribute the ten points, giving no more than four points to an item. Example:

DENISE Item	SAHIB Item
A 2	A 1
B	B 1
C	C 2
D	D
E 4	E 3
F 4	F 2
G	G 1

3. **Deal with the results.** Be prepared to be surprised. The outcome is likely to reveal consensus or provide a quantum leap in that direction.

Note: Too much talk about alternatives can block out a near agreement with static. That's where the orchestra leader's listening and timing become critical. Figure out when it makes sense to ask for a show of hands to see how many members prefer a certain option that some of them keep harking back to. Or, in a group of five to eight, use the ten-point distribution technique to "get a sense of the meeting." Quite often you'll discover a near consensus that simply calls for a little more ribbon to the bow before you take a final, decisive snip.

Map F: Decision Making

This procedure assumes steps 1 to 7 in the problem-solving map above have been completed.

1. Draft a statement of each possible solution. Letter each statement so the numbering during force-ranking doesn't confuse matters.

2. Force-rank the solutions. Use a simple ranking of first choice, second choice, and so on; the ten-point distribution procedure; or another technique.

3. Circle or underscore "discordant parts." Focus only on those parts of the top-ranked statement about which opinions vary.

4. Rework the "discordant parts." Negotiate wording that allows everyone to come to consensus, perhaps merging parts of the top-ranked solutions.

FINCH: I don't want to slip into clichés, but I say: Get me an 85 percent or 90 percent solution now rather than a 100 percent solution in a month. I have this bias, based on experience, that it's very hard to determine the optimal solution. There could be multiple 100 percent solutions. But if you don't act in a timely manner, you're going to lose an opportunity.

Finally, when it comes to agreeing on a course of action, it helps to share this observation from Theodore Isaac Rubin, M.D., psychiatrist and author of *Overcoming Indecisiveness:* "Remember the Big Fact!. Recall it at least several times. Say it out loud: 'In very few instances is one decision actually better than another.' We must give up a number of choices, quit them, let them go, in order to invest ourselves in the choice or choices we make. The choice will become a good decision if we can dedicate ourselves to making it a good one!"

WALTON: Sometimes I have to make this point: We're not exploring and educating; we're coming to a resolution. We "explored" in previous meetings. Now we have one task: to make a decision.

---

gluttons at a cornfest

Maximizing efficiencies with well-timed handouts

At IBM, where he trained more than 8,000 sales representatives, David Peoples always reminded his charges, "If in doubt, have a handout." Good advice indeed.

Whether it be a piece of paper or a computer screen serving the same purpose as a handout, it should go a long way toward thinning the flab from a get-together—especially a teleconference or a videoconference—if it was prepared with these key questions in mind:

Who will be the chief audience for the handout?

What information should it provide?

Where will it fit into the overall message I want to convey?

When will be the best time to use it?

Why will the audience and I benefit from having it?

How will the handout ensure answers to the preceding five W's?

Giving the questions more than lip service saves attendees from coping with uninformative handouts about an unfamiliar topic or, conversely, information overload in a deluge of copy.

With three types of handouts—send-befores, give-ats, and take-aways—a number of such debacles can be avoided, not the least of which is drowning in a Niagara of talk, often indicated by sessions going on hour after hour, day after day, partly because no one anticipates—like the leader with the mind of a general contractor—the need for procedure maps and handouts.

Each type of handout is described here, including its possible purposes and contents, with its implicit messages about other things that can turn a listless meeting into a lively one. Critical dos and don'ts are also given. The general guidelines apply, of course, across the board.

GENERAL GUIDELINES

• Exploit the capabilities of outstanding software graphics packages.

• Examine your agenda for key words, especially the verbs (*compare, classify, select, draft, schedule*), to note hints for handouts.

• Work backward in making an agenda by toying with handouts when you are stymied about how to approach a problem-solving challenge or you find yourself overwhelmed by all you want to accomplish. Think: *What do group members need to discover, and how might those discoveries be facilitated by matrices or exercise worksheets? What might the documents look like? How might columns and headings help show relationships or surface understandings?*

As you fiddle around with layouts, you'll often get an Aha! yourself, usually for an idea likely to engage more of the participants and, at the same time, an idea that ultimately serves to focus the agenda.

• Assume the role of orchestra conductor and ask yourself: *Where might a handout serve best to change pace and rhythm? Where might one prompt debate? Where might a handout introduce a new theme?*

• Get that monkey off your back. Don't assume you yourself have to make the handouts. After all, it's every member's meeting, not just yours. Delegate, stimulate. Energize participants and build ownership in the process.

- Try to have a copier in the room or nearby to make handouts of transparencies, hard-copy sketches, and the like produced by team members during a session. An electronic copyboard can, in some cases, supplant the need for a copier.

- Make sure the recorder/publisher, if you intend to use one, knows which text to type up and which to run off in participants' longhand during a collaborative get-together. *Note:* A team member working with a laptop might serve a similar role.

- Three-hole punch the paper to retain documents, perhaps in a binder designed for that purpose.

Reference Cues

- Use a running header, footer, or both on a multi-page document. The header might consist of your name and phone number; the footer, a copyright notice if information is proprietary.

- Cite the date, showing day, month, year. Also stamp the hour whenever versions of a document change that quickly.

- Title the handout for another quick reference point, especially when considering the handout a potential part of a report.

- Number the pages. Or, if the pages contain text with numbered lines, perhaps label the pages A, B, C, and so on.

- Use the numbering and lettering conventions of outlining only when they serve a handout well. Most outlined points are elliptical, delivering little or no meaning unless they have been annotated.

- Attach an explanatory or instructional cover note whenever appropriate. Don't simply dump and run, for nothing'll get done.

- Use colored paper; but on a multi-page handout, use it for the first page only. Nothing is more frustrating than trying to eyeball an item in a blizzard of white.

WALTON: In a meeting I ran a while ago, I color-coded my handouts and sent them out as advanced reading material. Color-coding them to correspond with instructions and empha-sizing that they would not be reviewed at the meeting made people take the warning seriously.

Illustrations

- Think first of an illustration, then the text. Though the sequence may not always be possible or appropriate, it often produces a document that's more helpful to your own understanding as well as that of colleagues.

- Caption and annotate illustrations to help ensure common understandings and to avoid rambling explanations during a meeting.

- Use the same typeface and type size to denote comparable parts of an illustration. Otherwise readers become confused.

- Use color on a drawing to clarify a complicated set of relationships. If the drawing is expected to be reproduced for pass-on readers, also consider the cost of colored copies versus what understandings might be lost through black-and-white reproductions.

Text

- Provide clear and concise copy. Avoid jargon if possible; define terms when necessary.

- Double- or triple-space copy to be critiqued, edited, or both.

- Number, at the left, lines of a document likely to demand scrutiny. What a lard-licker the numbers become as participants begin to say things like "I have a concern about lines 8 to 12 on page C" or "Will everyone please turn to page 4 and look at line 19? I believe we need to convey greater urgency from there to line 23."

- Use brief paragraphs, headings, and other typographical devices to speed reading.

- Target the immediate audience but, when appropriate, also consider pass-on readers, some of whom may be potential JIC-Ps you'd like to keep barricaded in their bins.

SEND-BEFORES

Note: GTE clients of mine look to these kinds of documents to "jump-start" a meeting, to avoid diddling around on matters that can be done offline beforehand. A three-dimensional mock-up or a rapid prototype can serve a similar purpose.

PHILLIPS: The use of jump-start documents can reduce a team's work from months to weeks or a week to a day. A key is having the right experts contribute to or confirm the content of the jump-start before using it within the team. Also, I find there's tremendous value in distributing the document ahead of time. Then people can digest the material and come prepared. They can get input from colleagues who have additional knowledge or are key to empowering team members to "buy in" to the solution or decision.

Purposes

- to establish a mindset about tone, direction, and import of the meeting
- to help maintain alignment
- to give members an opportunity to submit agenda items
- to update topics missed or affected since last meeting
- to provide background on new topics
- to provide "gray squirrel" introverts a chance to reflect
- to assign preparatory tasks for streamlining a meeting
- to eliminate or minimize potential JIC-Ps
- to provide names, numbers, addresses
- to expedite a teleconference with visual aids

Contents

- agenda, including the list of prospective participants
- template for submitting an agenda item (see page 21)
- charter or mandate
- copies of a contract, policy, practice, procedure
- a list of intended deliverables
- Q&A backgrounder on a topic to be addressed in the meeting
- a straightforward narrative about a topic
- pertinent articles or excerpts from them
- a jump-start position paper, schematic, definition, or the like
- an annotated problem statement
- key terms and acronyms with definitions

- results from a survey demanding scrutiny
- brochures, spec sheets, photos of three-dimensional mock-ups
- numbered "talk-to" points for participants in a teleconference
- autobiographical sketches or questionnaires completed by members of a long-term task force assembling for the first or second time
- templates completed from those listed on page 65

WUNDERLIN: Sometimes we're asked to quote on "How much would it cost to provide an interface between this system and that?" Well, with that kind of request, there are about 3,000 questions you want to ask. So we've developed templates and checklists to manage expectations.

Dos

- Be as user-friendly as possible.
- Include a cover note.

1. Emphasize that the pre-meeting tasks are aimed not only at giving people time to think and reflect but to speed the meeting itself.

2. Tell the purpose of each handout and what is to be done with it.

3. Cite deadlines for turnarounds and explain the importance of meeting the deadlines.

4. Remind participants the get-together will be run on the assumption that all pre-meeting tasks have been completed.

Don'ts

- Don't overwhelm participants to the point of resistance.
- Don't ramrod an issue—or even think of doing so!

The body of a cover note—electronic or hard copy—might say something like this, with "level-setting" referring to the objective of "getting everyone on the same plane of understanding" (See page 144).

Sometimes you may need to distribute a pre-meeting packet. If so:

1. Put the items in a pocketed portfolio.

2. Attach a brief cover note.

COVER NOTE TO HANDOUTS

These three documents will help streamline Thursday's meeting.

A. Agenda: Please note the time allotments.

B. Draft of position paper: (1) Underline any confusing copy and (2) fax me your marked copy on or before 1/7 so I can consider everyone's markings and incorporate them in a revision to be distributed at the meeting.

C. Article from "Water Resources Bulletin": Read for level-setting.

To ensure our customers are well served by an efficient and effective get-together—and in fairness to teammates—I'll assume you will have completed all instructions above.

Note: Put copies of all items in your binder and bring with you.

---

3. Include an annotated table of contents citing the title—and sometimes the color—of each handout, the purpose for which it is included, and any instructions the team member needs to complete before convening.

Whichever form the pre-meeting materials take, let them make participants say to themselves, *Gee, it looks as if we're going to get something done; I don't want to miss it!*

GIVE-ATS

Purposes

- to serve as an alternative to a transparency of a procedure map
- to provide a tracking guide for overhead flimsies, a speaker's key points, or the like
- to involve members by having them complete parts of a document
- to deal with statistics, e.g., spreadsheets that cannot be projected without resembling an ant colony
- to let each member have copies of items made on the spot during a meeting

Note: Often the most worthwhile give-ats are made and reproduced during a meeting. They aid tracking, help individuals who are more visual than auditory in their learning styles, and serve as a common space for participants to share—a major point elaborated on in the next chapter.

Contents

- a numbered set of key questions paralleling the parts of a presentation, with white spaces provided as prods to active listening and note-taking
- a jump-start schematic, matrix, or the like held in abeyance until the proper time
- important information gleaned from index-card responses, particularly assumptions aired on the group's "clothesline" (page 37) or ice-breakers revealing participant's values and interests (page 35)
- hard copy of pictorial images from transparencies or 35mm slides to be annotated
- a skeletal, *sentence* outline of a presentation to facilitate note-taking and to provide an understanding of the dominant message even to pass-on readers not attending the meeting
- annotated illustrations; charts, graphs, or the like; agendas for breakout groups
- worksheets to be completed, perhaps, by breakout groups
- templates and completed samples to guide group writing
- feedback sheets for evaluating a meeting as well as a presentation or related event (see pages 60 and 176)
- printouts from a copyboard, primarily consisting of sketches participants annotate as a meeting progresses from that point on

Dos

- Be sure to follow the General Guidelines cited earlier because many are critical for give-ats.
- Make more copies than you think you'll need, for JIC-Ps sprout faster than mushrooms in a compost heap.
- Take the "news" out of a handout by announcing it before you distribute the document; and, if desirable, allow participants to survey a multi-page give-at before you navigate them through it.
- Distribute portions of a handout to control and direct the attention of participants, even if it means doling out a page at a time and stapling sets of pages later. The technique can also offer a welcome change of pace.
- Consider making give-ats interactive by requiring participants to fill in blanks, complete a bar graph, or perhaps answer items on a humorous quiz while you wrap oral commentary around a pertinent point, pen in an element on a projected image, or both.

- Strive to make each projection in a presentation feature a pictorial image with only a key word or two, so hard copy of the images or their reduced facsimiles can be annotated by participants as they listen to a well-paced narrative that allows for the tactile reinforcement of key points.

  Note: Among the major wasteful-meeting breeders are hard-copy handouts from a overhead presentation in which bulleted phrases serve as prompts for a speaker (probably the most common type of projection). If the hard copy has not been annotated well—or not at all—the meaning of the handout virtually disappears with the flick of the projection lamp. Thus, when participants refer to the copy again—if it doesn't simply sit and collect dust or get heaved into the shredder—they have little or no accurate recall of the content. To pass-on readers it might just as well be ancient Urdu!

  In either case, the copy may become the initial whispers in the game of "Gossip," or, if ignored altogether, it might impede an important project. The safest thing is to provide a take-away as well, one consisting of the reproductions of five or six annotated slides revealing the heart of a presentation story. In short, do whatever you can to ensure no distortion of facts as such materials get passed on, especially if you want to deter the potential seat-warming JIC-Ps. Also, understand that handout facsimiles of projections with complete sentences read by a presenter are insults to audiences, and a guaranteed turn-off if there are so many words the screen swarms with locusts.

- Tell participants how and when you'll respond to questions about a handout. Often it is best to say, "Please use this document to take notes as I go along. After the presentation, I'll answer any questions." If you don't proceed this way, you run the risk of digressions caused by premature questioning—fat you can't afford!—and the impact of your presentation gets lost.

- Compile, from meeting to meeting, copies of matrices, guidelines, or the like that you can quickly retrieve and reproduce for handouts, either from a diskette or a master kept in your Facilitator's Handbook.

Don'ts

- Don't make hard copy of slides or transparencies consisting mainly of bulleted phrases only. The video generation prefers pictures; besides, the messages they convey linger longer.

- Don't vie with the *Congressional Record* for the Bluster & Blubber Award.

TAKE-AWAYS

Purposes

- to provide the all-important, motivating message that the meeting resulted in something of value—and preferably something tangible the participants helped create
- to reinforce topics covered in the meeting by presenting information in a format that may appeal to learning styles not previously accommodated
- to highlight key understandings, assignments, and so on
- to help maintain a gap-free project record that can refresh the memory, update an alternate, or both

Contents

- a sketch representing a discovery—a shared understanding—that grew out of collaboration
- important text from selected index cards, easel sheets, and transparencies reproduced during a meeting
- printouts made from a copyboard that require further reflection and deliberation—what one client refers to as mood food—for the "gray squirrel" introverts who, during the meeting, might have reacted negatively to proclamations from extroverted "polar bears"
- a record of action items written in longhand (perhaps on a transparency), reproduced on a nearby copier, and distributed before adjourning an ad hoc get-together
- a Q&A document reiterating key points made in a presentation
- a draft of a report or similar deliverable produced by members during a meeting
- selected images from a presentation that have been reproduced and annotated for clear recall of the main message, for pass-on readership, or both
- a set of minutes reflecting key understandings that grow out of the meeting (see page 107)
- printouts of an action-plan matrix filled in on a copyboard as tasks are assigned during a meeting

Dos

- Make each a stand-alone, reader-appealing piece.

- Remember that you can quickly reproduce easel sheets and similar items by taping them to a copyboard before pressing the printout button.

Don'ts

- Don't refer early to a prepared take-away that might spur immediate demand for it and thus destroy the rhythm and momentum of your intentions.
- Don't let a meeting adjourn without a take-away—one that not only connotes results and progress but engenders enthusiasm for ensuing work.

<table>
<tr><td>

13

</td><td>

morphing at Maloney's

</td></tr>
</table>

Achieving breakthroughs by sketching and sharing space: the surprising secrets to productivity gains

In a collaborative meeting, it's not so much the tools that matter; it's how we use them. And as the following two scenes illustrate, there's a world of difference.

SCENE ONE: LA PRETENSE BISTRO

Adlai and Ilona, computer-bonded for the first time by Egads, the Matchmaker, are sitting in a banquette at a linen-draped table with silver place settings, paper napkins, and a bud vase with plastic rose. The funereal air and stiff waiter do nothing to ease the tension. The chemistry between them, a tepid H_2O, simply isn't working.

Uncomfortable, Adlai starts to doodle on his napkin. Ilona inquires, "May I ask what that is?" "Nothing much," he answers, "just a little something I'm working on back at the office."

"Hmm . . . interesting," she replies, forcing a Mona Lisa and rescued by the arrival of the chateaubriand "with our deelicious house sauce," the waiter sniffs, "salmon de Rive Colorado."

Minutes later, Monsieur Dominique, the major domo, pops out from behind a trellis and heads their way. He's just burst from the kitchen, where the chef was in a snit and the wine steward tried chasing Dominique into the meat locker. But quickly the domo regains his composure, tugs at his formal, and snaps to a manner á la Pretense—for he must never betray the behind-the-scenes trappings or chaos. He offers a patronizing comment. Adlai nods. Ilona manages a perfunctory smile.

Finally, during les bananas bombé, the garcon commits a faux paux of les grande proportions: He dribbles café on the white linen, right next to the plastic rose. The hawk-eyed domo leaps from his perch and goes ballistic! Patrons stop and stare. Every waiter in the place shivers with fear. "You know what I eekpect!" shrieks the enraged Dominique. "Eeef I've told you once, I've told you ayzeeelion times. . . ."

In the melée, Adlai and Ilona break for the beads of the portiére—doing a sort of a demi-dash so as not to look indecorous or to clatter the plastic baubles. For a few seconds they were embarrassed voyeurs. Now they're secretly delighted and relieved: no more La Pretense, no more strained pleasantries, no more pressures of a next commitment. Adlai shakes Ilona's hand. She says, "Thank you, Adlai. It was a pleasant evening." And as they go their separate ways, each is thinking, Wait till I see that Egads!

SCENE TWO: THE CORNER GRILL

The place is a hubbub of noontime activity. At the center of the restaurant is an open grill, where the chef and assistants are bantering back and forth while juggling orders. At a dart board in a game corner, Vic and Jerry are engaged in their usual diversion. Maloney, the proprietor, has dropped by the players and is enjoying a belly laugh under his leather apron.

Waiters and waitresses are scurrying among the tables circling the grill. Meg and Rob are hovering over a square covered with off-white butcher paper. Meg is penciling something. Rob asks, "Is that what you were telling me about when I met you at the conference Tuesday?"

"Uh-huh," says Meg, "but right now I'm hung up on this part." She taps it.

"*Hmm . . . what about this?*" *Rob suggests, as he takes his ballpoint and adds a figure that looks like a piece of Swiss cheese.*

"*Ooh, I think you're onto something,*" *Meg responds. "I wonder if. . . . " And within minutes the two turn their table top into a contraption of inverted saucers, utensil-vectors, and intersecting red and green circles drawn with crayons from the tin cup next to the sugar packets.*

During the brainstorm, the ubiquitous Maloney grabs a handful of toothpicks at the checkout register. "These might help," he offers. And Stella, everybody's favorite waitress, gets involved after she accidentally spills some pea soup on the paper. Meg exclaims, "Look, that may be the shape of the keystone mechanism!" And with a daisy that Rob plucks from the fresh bouquet in a tiny sprinkling can and radiates over the splotch, the couple continue to reshape and study their design, happily building on a wisecrack from good ol' Stella when she tries to find room for the chicken Caesars.

Meg hails her office podmates: "Hey, Victoria, Jerry, come here." She tells them about the model, and Rob clues them in on the sticklers. That leads the four to head for the chalk and oversized tote board in the game corner. And before the lunch hour ends, many of the Corner Grill regulars also find themselves in the midst of the give-and-take, with heated arguments adding to the flavor.

(The lights fade and rise again, indicating a passage of time.)

As Vic and Jerry enter, Maloney bellows, "Hey, guys, how are your buddies, Meg and Rob? Haven't seen them for a while."

"*Getting along great,*" *Victoria answers. "Haven't you heard?" Jerry adds. "Today they're filing for a patent."*

CLOSE ONE, FRANCHISE THE OTHER

Though the contrasts are stark (and slightly overdrawn to make the point indelible), the meeting environment of the bistro typifies what skillions of meeting participants complain about: an environment with temperamental bosses and well-intentioned employees working in a swirl of unknown, conflicting, or unreasonable expectations; task-force appointees thrust together by remote delegators ignorant of a group's intent; one-way transmittal of information; compartmentalized mentalities and ghettoized participants; and even a troublemaker or two who, despite subject-matter specialties, should be filleted and broiled. Unless it opted to open for occasional briefings or low-budget dog-and-pony shows, this type of gathering place could provide the best of services by bolting its door and telling the world: Leaving Town. Going Out of Business!

Hearing such news, frequenters of the Corner Grill would shout *Ole! Vive la difference!* For Maloney's lair is a meeting place virtually everyone enjoys and thrives in, from the manager and chef to employees and customers. Not only is the environment physically open—even the headquarters with the COO and staff is visible—but so are the relationships, evidenced by how the characters flow in and out of situations with comfort and ease. It's a place where meeting participants take advantage of the ambiance and available tools, transforming it into a clubhouse of collaboration. It's the kind of gathering spot that should go into immediate, widespread franchising with this promotional pitch: Free! Secret Recipes Upon Request.

Camouflage and Anvils

A chief secret—and a highly symbolic one as well—lies in the difference between Adlai's solitary doodle on the napkin and Meg and Rob's interactive use of the butcher paper.

Adlai's drawing—the napkin's primitive equivalent to an overhead projection, a computer-screen graphic, a videotape, a faxed illustration—goes nowhere. Sending a strictly one-way message, Adlai uses the tool in the same way millions of other message-senders do. Meanwhile, receivers of the message, like Ilona and her countless counterparts, simply sit and take in bits and pieces of the information—if that. Furthermore, if they find no personal benefit in the data or display little curiosity in whether it might have value ("Hmm . . . interesting"), one thing is certain: Little of significance will be accomplished if more than mere exposure to the information is expected.

Most of the time, though, more *is* expected. But the expectations are unfortunately thwarted by poor use, misuse, or abuse of tools in an environment antithetical to honest-to-goodness give-and-take. Many meetings fail because the appearance of two-way communication is really camouflaging what is one-way only, thus perpetuating a cycle born out of frustration and ignorance of the basic problem. No wonder the weight of meetings turns organizations into anvils.

Morphing of Minds Meeting

From the moment Meg and Rob start to sketch on the butcher paper, they are sharing space. And as Michael Schrage of MIT points out, "It takes shared space to create shared understandings."

At the Corner Grill, the paper-covered table is like the "stage" of an overhead projector. But Meg doesn't simply sketch one thing or do a series of sketches as if they were "builds" in a one-way, overhead presentation. Instead, Rob enters the space with his comments and ballpoint additions. That invasion alters not only the physical landscape of the butcher paper but also the mental landscape—what each is thinking. It's as if Rob had put a blank overlay on a projection by Meg and sketched on it, or he had shared space by scribbling a note on a fax Meg had sent him and then returned it so that she, back in her office, could adjust the physical model (another shared space) on which both of them were mentally working.

Moreover, with the saucers and crayons, knives and forks, toothpicks and tote board, plus the advice of consultants who enter and leave the space in one way or another, Meg and Rob keep experiencing shifts in the terrain—both physical and mental—out of which grows an idea neither could have generated independently.

By using the tools to create a collaborative environment—enhanced further by the openness of the room and the people in it—the participants at the Corner Grill get-together begin to fuse their minds into a communal brain. Its effect in many ways resembles the morphing seen in movies and TV

SUNDY: We're in a lab complex, with a bunch of rooms off a common hallway. Chalkboards and whiteboards line the hall. If I were to walk down the hallway and run into my lab mentor, I might say, "Hey, let me show you this. Here's some data I found." I might draw a table that prompts other ideas and discussion.

So the stuff you might see on a chalkboard might be an outline of different experiments or different priorities or different diagrams trying to understand a particular biological phenomenon. They will remain after the conversation has ended. Some pieces of conversation will last on the board for maybe a half hour. I also can think of one schema we've had for three months now. Every now and then, I'll refer to it by going around the corner in the hall and looking at it briefly to see if it might help what I'm doing, if it'll jog my memory.

---

commercials, where a lotus blossom, for instance, melts into a tiger that dissolves into a jet that transforms into the skyline of nighttime Hong Kong. At the Corner Grill, individual minds morph into one huge, collective brain. *Thus, the event is not so much a meeting of minds as it is the morphing of minds meeting.*

And in most kinds of meetings, achieving that special effect is what a good leader and team strive to do.

ETCH A SKETCH

One of the fastest ways to begin the morphing—and ultimately peel away layers of meeting fat caused by delayed understandings, misunderstandings, and so on—is to urge participants to put a sketch at the center of deliberation as soon as possible. Or, if a member of a group has background on the subject of an upcoming get-together and knows its purpose, encourage him or her to bring a "jump-start schematic." The latter can be a simple, clean one done by hand, a more intricate one produced with software, or a quick-sketch produced on the spot. Whichever, it will do one or more of the following:

- **Unshackle those who think alphanumerically only.** Sketching becomes another language, another tool that frees and enables collaborators. It's like offering someone who has traveled only by car and train the option and advantages of traveling by plane.

> DUENOW: Clients are always impressed with sketches. They help people articulate what they *don't* like. Whereas if they had to articulate that in some other way, you wouldn't hear it or hear it precisely. But you have to be careful. You can give people too much of an idea, and they latch onto it as fact. Then they talk too much about that sketch, rather than the concept it represents. The process becomes counterproductive. The sketch has to be brought in at the right time.

- **Vary the rhythm, pace, and quality of deliberation.** Rather than sit, sit, sit as they talk, (via monologue) talk, talk, yawn, talk, yawn, yawn à la Pretense, most participants in a Maloney-like world become involved in a meeting when, as interacting individuals, they stand-to-sketch, sit, talk (via dialogue) stand-to-sketch, sketch some more, sit, talk, final-sketch—or vary the sequence in any of its endless, yawnless ways.

• **Give participants something they can visualize and then verbalize.** Deliberation is often streamlined by a flow chart, a cross-sectional diagram, a jerry-rigged model like Meg and Rob's—because it is easier for most people to grasp the relationship of the parts to the whole, a capability particularly important when the whole comprises something complicated and dynamic. (Try explaining, in words only, how an eggbeater works. Get the picture?)

It is important to recognize, however, that sometimes a significant amount of talk must occur to achieve level-setting among participants before anyone can begin to glimmer a potentially helpful sketch. Once, for instance, it took two-and-a-half days of discussion and several sketches—via pads, superimposed transparencies, and a software package—before three labeled, concentric circles, with the smallest a solid bull's-eye, proved to be a major Aha! on a cross-functional task force—a shared understanding gained by the morphing of minds.

COWLEY: Sometimes on a very complex project, I'll start to sketch something. Then the client will pick up a pen and start to go at it, which to me seems at first to add to the confusion. But it somehow solidifies in the client's mind what he or she really wants, and then the client understands *my* diagram better.

• **Frame a concrete space that can be shared literally.** After an illustration has been presented on an overhead transparency, people might mark directly on it, perhaps using different colored pens to help the communal brain grasp other relationships, possibilities, understandings.

Sometimes people might show alternatives to a sketch by superimposing blank overlays on the original and marking them. Or they might juxtapose alternative drawings by using a second projector—an excellent technique for comparing and contrasting particularly complicated concepts. At the Corner Grill, the table top and tote board serve cruder but similar functions.

The technique also helped members of a committee who were struggling to decipher the fundamental difference between the positions *talked about* by a pair of respected specialists, one of whom had flown 1,500 miles to the meeting.

(Imagine how long and costly a filibuster that might have become!) Time was telescoped, however, by having the pair "duel with drawings" on twin projectors, with the foot-wide separation between the screens literally providing the only physical break in the shared space. During the illustrated debate, one of the observers "morphed in," verbalized what she discovered as the chief difference, and thereby led her colleagues to gain the same insight.

During the course of a get-together someone might also sketch on a electronic copyboard, encourage others to doodle with the graphic, then make printouts for offsite Subject Matter Specialists (SMEs), with a cover note about suggesting additions and corrections via phone call, fax, or e-mail. Some respondents might also choose to offer a completely new illustration—and space—for the communal mind to explore.

CAMERON: I think we live by schematics in a lot of ways. We diagram 'em out. We use overhead projectors to scribble on, or whiteboards, fax machines, or those blackboards that copy themselves. In most cases, our people rely on pencils and paper and blackboards. If we have a meeting of a seven-person crew and are working on a problem, we're focused on the *problem*; we don't have time to make up fancy slides and things.

WUNDERLIN: Last week I came to a point in a teleconference where, if I had been in a face-to-face meeting, I would have walked up to a copyboard and sketched. Instead, I drew on a piece of plain white paper with circles, squares, and arrows and faxed it to the customer. It was amazing how fast we continued.

Surprising Interplay

Illustrations can also provide an effective vehicle for an individual to interact with others. In the following cases, for example, sketching was used to:

- **Create a stimulator, incubator, motivator.** A jump-start schematic can stimulate (prod externally) someone to incubate a concept and then become motivated (prodded internally) to offer a revision or a fresh start.

  After a day of level-setting, in which a task force came to a shared understanding about a problem as well as the minimum criteria a solution had to meet, I suggested the participants break into three groups. Each was challenged to rough out a schematic showing a solution. After 30 minutes, the groups reconvened and presented their overhead projections. Two approaches looked like Mondrian imitations and the third, a Rube Goldberg, but none completely satisfied the task force. They had run out of steam. So hard-copy sets of the schematics were distributed, and the members adjourned for the evening.

That night, Ellen, an out-of-town member staying at the hotel, kept flipping through the roughs. (Imagine if hard copies had *not* been made!) Even during her dinner, she kept reflecting (an act more likely induced by the quiet of a La Pretense) and red-penning the handout (as would be virtually expected at the grill). Then, instead of dessert, Ellen had a Eureka! She dashed back to the meeting room, grabbed some fresh transparencies, and amalgamated portions of the alternatives into a new drawing with overlays. Next day, Ellen's schematic and explanation were greeted with applause, signaling not only the group's appreciation but also their collective Aha! And the meeting, with momentum on a roll again, soon sped to a close.

- **Encourage a person struggling with language to find the right words.** That was Bill's problem during another meeting I led, in which he offered a challenge to his colleagues: "Please listen to what I'm having a hard time trying to convey, and see if any of you can draw it." After Bill went through his explanation, a team member sketched an interpretation. Then, with just a few tweakings, everyone in the room who had been sharing the mental space, including Bill, finally discovered the exact words for what he wanted to say. And what a boon that eventually proved in condensing the group's final report, which consisted mainly of the illustration and the precise wording Bill had brought about.

Effects on Dynamics

It's also fascinating to observe how the "concreteness" of a sketch can:

- **Thwart incorrigible troublemakers.** As long as a meeting consists of talk, talk, talk, it's pretty easy for the likes of Doomsayer, Vacillator, and Intimidator to ply their trades. But once a schematic is at the center of discussion, it usually encourages a larger number of people to speak up with confidence and specificity, because they have something tangible to respond to.

- **Force a hand of cards—or at least allow a good peek.** The phenomenon previously described can also flush out the person who plays his or her cards close to the chest. When a pivotal schematic is being dealt with and engenders not only animated discussion but also movement toward an end that doesn't favor the card holder's hidden agenda, you'll hear stammerings of objections and offerings of what-ifs and how-abouts. All, of course, are clues to the speaker's agenda, giving consensus-builders something to grab hold of in appealing to the person's concerns, values, or both.

A Document Thinner

Reports and such also become far less imposing as participants begin to think more naturally in pictures and do the following:

- **Play detective with a storyboard.** As committee members examine a storyboard, they will, from time to time, see where intended gobs of copy for a report can be replaced by one or more illustrations. Without the storyboard, detecting the incipient fat-producers is hard, if not impossible. What's more, if someone writes and becomes emotionally wedded to the copy, hours of wordsmithing can turn progress into a rhino wallow.

  The attempt at illustration can also reveal gaps and overlaps in the embryonic narrative—the potential canyons and turnoffs that stop readers who get lost or bored.

- **Slim-trim the tomes.** The old adage "a picture is worth a thousand words" comes into play again. Often a task-force report—the shared space at the center of group writing (see Chapter 15)—need only include captioned and annotated illustrations, plus verbiage pertaining to conclusions and recommendations.

GETTING MINDS TO MORPH

See for yourself, for I can't stress enough the power of the picture. Whether you work with computers and groupware or, like the majority of meeting-goers, still prefer easel sheets and overhead transparencies, bring to your get-togethers the concepts of morphing, the sharing of space. With those ideas at the forefront of your brain, consider the following questions as you plan and handle the meetings:

- **If the gathering requires collaboration, e.g., planning, brainstorming, problemsolving, decision making, how can I create an environment more like the grill than the bistro?** Start with the right perspectives, the right attitudes.

In some cases, where the information flow has to be one-way for the intended purpose of the gathering (e.g., a new employee orientation or a low-key campaign kickoff), the listen-from-your-cubicle aspects of La Pretense might be perfectly fine. Don't presume, either, that the more convivial atmosphere of the grill is unprofessional; at times, fun and silliness—even happy accidents—are sources of significant insights and breakthroughs.

- **Do I realize and respect the fact all of us in the group will be embarking on a process of discovery?** In an effective collaborative meeting, participants act very much like writers, taking hints and fragments of understandings and drafting and redrafting and redrafting (cf., sketching, dialoguing, morphing) to discover what it is they have to say. "We do not write in order to be understood," said C. Day Lewis, "we write in order to understand."

> "People sometimes talk of me as a lone inventor. Nonsense! Where would I have been without [my laboratory assistants] Charles Batchelor and John Kruesi and all the others? We worked long hours together, and nobody ever had a better time."
>
> *Thomas Edison*

That attitude, with its underlying challenges, should not only be at the center of your planning but at the heart of the meeting itself, where morphing minds lead to the Ahas! of shared understandings. The process can be sloppy—even pocked with argumentative fits and starts. That's why it's painful for the Dominiques of the business world. Their unrealistic expectations and exhortations about "getting it right the first time" can, when interpreted literally, run counter to the discovery process. As a result, the rock-solid foundation of a good decision based on the morphing of minds is replaced by the quick fixes of shanties on sticks.

- **How can I work with an assortment of minds—each representing different strengths and perspectives—so when they morph, the communal brain is**

159

likely to provide potential for a depth and richness that might not otherwise be achieved? Although Ilona and Adlai threatened to wring the neck of Egads, they probably won't. In the end, they'll lack the energy and gumption. Besides, they'll prefer deriving pleasure from the fiasco by telling others what a gigantic waste of time the meeting was and how those other guys couldn't get their act together. In fact, Adlai and Ilona are likely to pop up again and again at the bistro, albeit in the tossed salads of other delegators, but with similar results. And that's why, unfortunately, the kinds of get-togethers that take place at La Pretense will continue, changing little from the snail-n-wail rituals held there under previous managements and designations: Charade and La Grande Illusion.

Imagine, however, if Ilona and Adlai were brought together with Meg and Rob at the Corner Grill. Or perhaps just Ilona on one occasion, Adlai on another. And people began to discover that Adlai was a local genealogy buff, and Ilona was a gamester and former pool hustler. Better still, picture what might happen if that subject-matter specialist, Stella, and Maloney himself joined a morphing? Yeoww! What depth, what richness!

• **What can I use for a jump-start schematic?** That, of course, depends on your type of work, as shown in the following:

POSSIBLE JUMP-START SCHEMATICS

Analysis of problem	Tentative layout of brochure
Possible solution	Floor plan
Flow chart	Ideal product, service
Process map	Rapid prototype
Geographical map	Organizational chart
Timeline	Photograph
Analogous drawing (e.g., an	Pie chart segmenting customer
organizational view akin to a	expectations, categories of
topographical map, with rivers,	complaints, focus group
mountains, islands, and so on)	suggestions, or the like

• **Should I think about shared space as I make an agenda for a collaborative meeting?** Although discoveries may lead a group to abandon some shared spaces (e.g., the butcher paper, temporarily) or exploit others (e.g., the tote board) along the way, always be alert to people conducting serial monologues (á la Pretense). Try to avoid that situation by thinking of sequences like the one below, then building a verb-spurred agenda from it. Each boldface word or phrase represents a shared space:

1. Brainstorm a tentative **storyboard.**

2. Draw a jump-start **sketch on an overhead transparency.**

3. Change the **storyboard** based on the **sketch.**

4. Hear and interrogate the speaker on the meeting subject, with the **room** providing the shared space of listeners.

5. Change the **sketch** and **storyboard** to reflect the changes brought about by the presentation and follow-up deliberation.

6. Watch a videotape on the subject, gaining insights that affect the **sketch.**

7. Hold a teleconference with the headquarters sponsor to get answers to key questions that also modify the **sketch,** a copy of which has been faxed to the sponsor.

8. Re-examine the **sketch** and alter it, if necessary, perhaps with participants working on overlays.

9. Call in SMEs for feedback about the **sketch,** which perhaps has been turned into copies of a more polished **hard-copy handout,** complemented by a **reference transparency of the sketch** for "blow-up" and revision as needed.

10. Alter the **storyboard** in light of steps 6 to 9, which were related to the **sketch.** Then conduct group writing of a report with a **master draft** as shared space (see Chapter 15). Refer as needed to the **storyboard** and the **handout of the completed sketch,** which is eventually melded into the final draft.

Note: In an ad hoc meeting, two or three people might produce a flow chart on an electronic copyboard and then make a printout for each person to study and mark up during adjournment. When the group reconvenes, they can share the space of each colleague's revised printout, which might also have been turned into an overhead transparency or an enlarged document for a more open and flexible shared space.

- **If I'm not already his clone, what does it take in a "Corner Grill meeting" to be a no-phony Maloney?** A lot more than it does to be a Dominique. Behind Maloney's casual manner lie the stalking sensitivities of a lion. Highly attuned to all that's going on, he's the kind of person who'd know exactly when to back off from Meg and Rob, how to ring in the COO and staff as their lunchtime pressures waned, when to surface an old-fashioned town hall debate, when and why to tap the wisdom of Vic or Jerry, and even if or when he might try calling those new customers from the bistro, Ad and Il.

Knowing the success of his business depends on fostering and maintaining amicable, fluid relationships among staffers, suppliers, repeat customers, new customers, and other participants in the various publics he serves, Maloney concentrates on those networks of relationships more than he does on the cost of beets and broccoli for the salad bar. Besides, the produce manager, Pilar, also eyeing the vision of the Corner Grill, will take care of that.

> "Manhattan is a narrow island off the coast of New Jersey devoted to the pursuit of lunch."
>
> Raymond Sokolov,
> "Design for Lunching"

This is not to say Maloney couldn't handle the salad bar or pinch-hit at the grill—for he's no slouch in the technical end of the business—but he knows where his priorities are and the constancy they demand. And as an "inspiring, aligning leader of all those with whom he gathers" (the Chamber's tribute), you'd find, if you were to ask him, that he developed most of his savvy, and continues to hone it, not through his MBA but through OJT: on-the-job-training.

Can't you just hear him? "Bag the case studies, buddy! Dive in and paddle like a duck in a downpour."

14 snorman norman & the knockemsockanovs

Ensuring that niche-pitched presentations serve a committee's wants, needs, and expectations

Candidates for a fat farm must include those endless, droning presentations by numerous consultants, suppliers, subject-matter experts, and other resources invited to address a committee. In newly reconfigured organizations, these people orbit in and out of task forces and cross-functional work teams, often sharing knowledge on the cutting edge of a topic to help a group in its discoveries and document-making. Unwittingly, however, many, through their presentations, lard a group's progress. You and I have not only seen these characters but—confess we must—we've even been them!

The Dazzlers: Executive producers of the Dog & Pony Show as well as easy marks for the latest in video gizmos, they don't realize that what they think communicates, obfuscates.

The Knockemsockanovs: They goose-step their way through a mechanistic routine "whether you like it or not!"

Ms. Flimsy: From a binder of 173 transparencies, she tries to tailor a presentation on the spot, while her distracting flips and clicks of the binder sound like Grandpa's loose choppers.

Rover & Co.: He and the other mutts sniff and paw the ground, leaving the head-scratching onlookers to wonder, *Was there* anything *to be found?*

Scrooge-Marner, Ltd.: Bean counters, they see everything through green eye shades, making overhead ledger sheets look like circuit boards.

Snorman Norman: While you're wondering about the potential markets for the invention, he's telling you about the shipping dates and the weight of the freighter that lugs the bauxite from Jamaica to Port Lavaca.

The Sieves: Despite the shelves of books they've read on how to give effective presentations, they violate every suggestion ever offered, following a speaker's version of what Charles ("On the Road") Kurault calls "the Victorian principle of furnishing: Too much is just right."

Good Ol' Gus: He's a great conversationalist down at the country store, but his hike-up-the-belt ramblings don't quite hack it in the executive suite.

Less than adequate performances by such individuals are not just of their own making; committee liaisons are to blame as well. And what could—and should—be well-framed, highly collaborative give-and-takes become presentations that hamper productivity by failing to convey needed information, concentrating more on the packaging and delivery of a message than on ways to ensure understandings that leave a dominant impression.

CAMERON: Analyzing your audience is very important. I just came from a presentation. I felt very uncomfortable because I didn't know who was going to be there. I was just told to show up to brief the Deputy Administrator on the mission. He was in from Washington [D.C.] for a meeting at the senior staff level. In this type of presentation, you've got important debrief items from a mission. Some are important at the operational level, some at the policy level. So you've got to sort out which ones are the right ones and be effective in making your recommendations. You must be technically competent and an excellent communicator.

To Serve the Committee Best

As either a meeting leader or a committee liaison who invites someone to address a group, your responsibility is to ensure that the speaker conveys and clarifies understandings fundamental to the group's common task. From the moment of notification, no matter how last-minute it may be, speakers should learn all they can about a committee and its objectives. If you extend invitations often, create a template like the one that follows. As a speaker yourself, adapt the template to suit that perspective, paying particular attention to scope, time constraints, purpose, and makeup of the audience.

MORE TIPS ON TALKS AFFECTING COMMITTEE WORK

For a talk affecting the work of a group and, in all likelihood, the document they're making, be sure these tips are followed as well—whether the speaker is someone else or you:

- **Realize no communication device—electronic or other—eradicates your need to accommodate a variety of viewpoints, levels of knowledge on a topic, individual learning styles, attention spans, and so on.** Know how and when to use the tools to share your own understandings as opposed to creating an environment in which people discover shared understandings. Each method has its time, place, and value. But be conscious of the differences as you plan a presentation to a committee, for their work will be influenced, to one degree or another, by what you and other resources provide. Aim less for cotton candy than for peanut butter clinging to the roof of the mouth.

- **Understand that many committees have to take your information, weigh it against what other experts say, and fit it into the bigger picture.** Because information in an arena of knowledge expands faster than they can absorb it, group members can't possibly keep up with all the details. Therefore, learning more about *context* helps them.

FINCH: A staff person needs to educate a decision-maker on the most relevant information, to help minimize uncertainty and risk. But if you can't collapse that information into key points, you don't really understand it. It's a difficult thing to do. It's difficult for *me*. It's hard work because you have to pick the right words to make the right points. A lot of people don't take time to think about those things.

PREPARATION GUIDELINES FOR A SPEAKER

Dear

How nice to know you'll be able to lend your expertise to our task force. To make sure the time you spend on your presentation benefits both you and the group, below is a "road map." It also serves as a checklist of points you and I may have discussed earlier or more informally. If there's anything else I can do for you, please call.

SUBJECT AND TIME ALLOTMENTS

You plan to address this topic: _____

Date: _____ Place: _____

Starting Time: _____ Stopping Time: _____

Committee members prefer an overview of approximately ____ minutes followed by an expansion of the overview for approximately ____ minutes, and a question-and-answer segment lasting approximately ____ minutes. The last segment is the longest to ensure that the most important concerns of the committee get expressed and addressed.

Note: Because the task force wishes to extend the same courtesies to all, scheduled speakers will not be left waiting or asked to abbreviate their planned remarks. When a speaker's time expires, committee members will submit queries on index cards for follow-up.

PURPOSE

The purpose of your talk will be to make sure the audience gains a clear understanding of the answers to the following major questions, which are central to the committee's task:

1. _____

2. _____

3 _____

4. _____

AUDIENCE Your audience will number _____ members, distributed as follows:

[ ] Finance   [ ] Info Technology   [ ] Marketing
[ ] Human Resources [ ] Manufacturing   [ ] Sales
[ ] _____   [ ] _____   [ ] _____

LIMITATIONS AND SUGGESTIONS

You do NOT need to cover the following topics because they are outside the scope of the committee's work:

_____   _____   _____

_____   _____   _____

Also, for this audience it would be advisable TO AVOID:

[ ] An emphasis on the *what* rather than the *why* of the what

[ ] A prepackaged, off-the-shelf sales pitch

[ ] Cluttered projections, especially those involving statistics

[ ] Projections with words only instead of annotated illustrations

[ ] Abstractions not explained through analogies, examples, mock-ups, diagrams, demonstrations, or the like

[ ] Jargon pertaining to _____

EQUIPMENT

The following will be available in the room:

[ ] Projection screen

[ ] Easel with pad

[ ] Slide projector

[ ] Overhead projector

[ ] VCR

[ ] Speakerphone 201-444-9773

[ ] LCD panel

[ ] Electronic whiteboard

[ ] Fax machine 201-444-8181

[ ]

[ ]

[ ]

If you need any other equipment, please contact _____ at phone number _____ or e-mail _____.

- **Picture a task force having to complete a jigsaw puzzle, one that results in a decision they reach, a report they write, a plan they devise.** Though your presentation represents only a piece of the puzzle, fitting it into place—helping the committee gain knowledge or flashes of insight—enhances your contribution, your value.

- **In a simple declarative sentence, write down the dominant message you intend to leave with the committee.** Then, after writing three or four key ideas that support the message, plan how to drumbeat them in as many sense-appealing ways as possible. To ensure retention, researchers say, a new message has to be experienced at least four to seven times—perhaps, for example, appealing to the eye with a striking image, to the ear with a catch phrase, to the hand with a demonstration or examination of a prototype.

- **Focus on oral language.** People are listening, not reading.

> PEEPLES: With one of our senior executives, I've told my staff members, "What you're going for [in a presentation] is to have his little head go up and down, up and down; that's the signal you're reaching him."

- **Link the points in your message to the committee's task, the benefits to the business, and the payoffs to the customer.** If you yourself can't see the critical interrelationships, don't expect your audience to.

- **With each point, keep asking:** *Why is it important? What images, tools, and exercises might I use to engage the committee, to make sure the point is understood, to make it stick?* By constantly focusing on the receivers of the message and striving for complete comprehension, packaging and delivery will practically take care of themselves. Beware, however, of overkill. "The best way to be boring," said Voltaire, "is to leave nothing out."

- **Think in pictures, pictures, pictures, for humans "can actually process visuals 60,000 times faster than text."** There isn't a business person alive who hasn't suffered through presentations by Great Yakkers tracking word-bugs on a screen; it's a fate worse than a medieval torture rack. So don't inflict such pain on others. At a minimum, resort to circles, lines, boxes, colors, and labels to show relationships and explain their functions. That's what a committee needs and wants to know, for behind any fancy dissolves or razzamatazz, the mental connections are all that really matter.

- **If words are necessary on a projection, use 18-point type in no more than two styles.** Also remember the 6 x 6 rule: no more than six lines per flimsy, and no more than six words per line.

- **Don't just slap-and-rap with an Eiffel Tower of transparencies.** Consider:

  —joining a colleague in a presentation dialogue, with the partner acting as a segment summarizer, for example, or playing "inquisitive customer" to your "supplier"

  —giving a lighthearted quiz at the beginning of a presentation to get the lay of the land

  —working with two overhead projection screens or one screen and an electronic copyboard, inviting committee members to respond to you in visual counterpoint

  —relating worksheets to a segmented presentation on a complicated topic

- **For most types of committees, avoid a presentation that's totally question-and-answer from the outset.** It's fraught with dangers, not the least of which is never getting the audience to grasp the gestalt, or big picture, of what you're trying to convey. At least give them that at the beginning— uninterrupted—and, if necessary, repeat it at the end. Or, if you wish, lay ground rules for your informal approach, making sure that built into the process are periodic summaries and a wrap-up.

- **Before giving an uninterrupted overview to a presentation, "name it and frame it."** That is, tell listeners what you plan to talk about and how you've structured the presentation to provide as clear an understanding as possible. Two examples:

  Here's how I've planned my presentation on "Utility Stocks with Lots of Ooomph!" For the first ten minutes, I'll give a quick overview. Then I'll open up for Q&A. If questions come to mind as I'm speaking—other than those about a word or phrase for which you need instant meaning—jot them down on index cards and ask them when the time comes.

In planning my talk on "Making Kilowatts from Kerosene" I've tried to keep this committee in mind. As with any of us giving a preso, I may, however, run the risk of not touching upon everyone's interest or concern. So I'd like to make this request: Please bear with me while I give about a 15-minute overview of the key message; then fire your questions. If you wish, write them on index cards so you won't forget them.

- **Allow for a question-and-answer period.** No matter how brilliant a performance you think you've given, if a committee member is left without his or her pet question addressed, you've fallen short of expectations in that person's mind. Don't end with Q&A, however. End with a brief recap.

- **Prepare a videotape, an audiotape, a Q&A handout, or perhaps all three devices if you find yourself giving essentially the same presentation over and over and over again.** Here are the advantages:
  If you're an in-house guru or specialist who feels like Silly Putty from all the committees tugging at you for your attention, you can take advantage of a less frantic pace to concentrate on the unique needs of each group, explore new territory, or both. In other words, you can indeed be in three, four, or more places at once if the same basic information is all that's being requested.

  By videotaping a good, serviceable presentation, you minimize the risk of misstating or omitting points in an extemporaneous wing-it, the seedbed of time-eroding spinoffs. No need, however, to Hollywood it for intra-company use or for clients and suppliers interested more in getting the information quickly and clearly than in evaluating production credits. Just splice and edit the tapes from a couple of initial presentations.

  For an audiotape to serve commuters, especially those traveling long distances or snailing in gridlock, simply adapt a Q&A handout, with a colleague-interviewer to provide a change of voice and pace. The handout can also serve either as a send-before (to save time on repeating points already understood or unimportant to a particular group) or as a take-away (to reinforce a message or ensure understandings you may not have time to convey in person).

METZGER: To me, face-to-face meetings, video conferences, and audio conferences are not mutually exclusive. They can be used together. In our business, a doctor who's a specialist in a particular field may send out a CD-ROM, video, or slide presentation to several locations. On the day of the audio conference, 200 or more may view the presentation at the same time as they're holding [on the audio conference hookup]. After they view the CD-ROM or video, the doctor gets on the line to answer questions. With slides, the speaker would actually narrate as each location views them.

BUT WHAT IF . . . ?

No matter how well you plan, there will always be speakers who need reminders and guidance till the very end of their presentations. These are the people who just don't seem to learn—like the robotic Knockemsockanovs.

In real life, they were from a blue-chip corporation and had been invited to a give a presentation to a committee I was facilitating. Their objective was to explain why their solution for a systems design warranted a highly prized contract.

Despite all my tips to halt their goose-steps for some give-and-take (the committee was ready to go out of its collective skull), the Marketing Commandant and his troops resisted every hint, no matter how firm or gentle. For their allotted hour, they never once took a suggestion or encouraged a question.

Following them was a lone speaker from another company who told the committee what he intended to cover, asked if his navigation plan seemed appropriate, acknowledged suggestions for adjustment, and proceeded with his overview. Then he double-checked for direction-setting cues ("Is this the kind of information you're interested in?"), completed his talk, and answered the members' queries.

Who won the award? Of course! The cocky Knockys were left hanging from the rope the committee had been only too happy to give them.

To prevent others from making fools of themselves, while also serving the needs of a task force, committee, or the like, consider the prompts that follow. As a meeting leader, you may need to use them—more often than not—with speakers who "still don't get it" and probably never will.

IF THE PRESENTER . . .	INTERJECT AND SAY . . .
Turns off the group by his or her excessive talk.	"Excuse me, Ralph, but I think if you could wrap up in the next minute or so and leave time for questions, you'll probably be able to cover the same points and yet be sure you've addressed everyone's concerns."
Uses an acronym or piece of jargon, as audience eyelids go south and subsequent understandings may be jeopardized.	"Is there anyone here who doesn't understand the term?" [Wait for a show of hands.] "Would you please explain it, Helen?"
Does not seem to be covering what the committee is searching for.	"Wally, let's be sure you're delivering what the committee needs." [PAUSE.] "How many are finding the information helpful so far? Please show by hands." [PAUSE.] "Are there any suggestions?"
Sifts gnats, reminiscent of Snorman Norman.	"Louise, that's all good information, but right now the group needs to see the big picture. Within the time remaining, I think it would help both you and the committee to emphasize *why* you think the solution is best. The group is already familiar with the nuts and bolts."

CHIEF LISTENER

When a speaker's topic promises to be as politically hot as cayenne pepper, appoint a chief listener, preferably someone with little or no stake in the subject.

Or it might be a person who, holding a strong adversarial view toward the topic, is forced to adjust his or her emotional filters and begin to gain insights that biases may have been screening. Complicated subjects can also benefit from the feedback of an official set of ears.

A listener might be appointed before a meeting or drafted at the last minute intentionally. In either case, instruct the person ahead of time or turn the steps below into a handout for on-the-spot guidance. After a team has worked together, the role becomes familiar. Rotating it also helps keep participants alert, slightly off center, involved.

Steps

Invite the chief listener to do the following on overhead transparencies at his or her seat:

1. Log in the date plus the speaker's name and subject at the top of the first transparency.

2. Number and capture each major point the speaker makes, but don't attempt to record copy verbatim.

3. Leave generous space after each entry.

   After the speaker has finished, ask the listener to:

4. Project the transparencies in sequence and either recap each item or have the speaker scan each numbered entry as it's pointed to. (Caution: Jumping around can land a group in a vat of fat!)

5. Urge the speaker—as well as team members—to deal with any misunderstandings, additions, omissions.

6. See that the corrected, longhand version of the approved transparencies is copied and distributed, perhaps as soon as the end of the next break.

   Note: An alternative procedure is to have the listener record the notes on paper or a laptop diskette and then meet with the speaker offline to determine their accuracy before making and distributing copies.

Advantages

- A publicly held follow-up, *limited to a few brief minutes*, creates an attention-getting, energizing dynamic.

- The speaker may make discoveries not only about things she thought she had said but also things she meant to say.

- Attendees who might have been mentally bobbing for apples during a presentation get another chance to catch salient points. Other participants might cite significant nuances that should not have been overlooked.

- Subsequent deliberation also benefits; clearing up misunderstandings before a guest speaker departs keeps listeners from getting mired in the swamps of I-Thought-She-Said.

- Copies of the notes provide a communal memory on a specific topic, a "database" team members can quickly tap for personal review, faxes to offsite associates, or other helpful purposes.

ACCOMMODATING BACK-TO-BACK SPEAKERS

Rather than have the whole group hear answers to questions that might only be of concern to certain interrogators, invite the latter to submit queries on index cards.

PHILLIPS: Hard copy of answers to questions on index cards serves as an audit trail. It minimizes confusion overall and can help inform others not attending the presentation.

Have the speaker follow up according to a plan previously agreed on. The product, for example, might be an informative Q&A document that has to meet a certain deadline to be of any value to the group's deliberation—and, in a number of cases, to the speaker's cause. Questions raised immediately after a presentation are more likely to benefit the whole group once individuals know they have a medium for getting their "personal concerns" addressed.

FEEDBACK ON A PRESENTATION

SPEAKER: _____ DATE: _____

TOPIC: _____

I. Complete each statement with ratings from the following key, and please be specific in your explanations.

KEY:
[3] Very Helpful [2] Helpful [1] Somewhat Helpful
[0] Not Helpful

A. In terms of its *relevance to our task*, the presentation was [ ]. Here's why:

B. In terms of *new learnings for me*, the presentation was [ ]. Here's why:

II. Put an X in the appropriate box.

A. The length of the talk was [ ] too long [ ] too short [ ] just right.

B. The speaker came across [ ] well prepared [ ] somewhat prepared [ ] poorly prepared.

III. Complete each statement with specifics, *including reasons for your comments*.

A. To me, the most valuable part of the presentation was:

B. I would like to have heard more about:

C. If the speaker were to address our group again, I'd recommend:

YOUR NAME: _____ PHONE: _____

Give 'em the Hook!

If a speaker does not complete a presentation on schedule and others are waiting, let the guidelines you set at the beginning about time limits and follow-up index cards come to the rescue. In a roster of back-to-back speakers, you must be ready to give "the hook" to any presenter, especially the first one, since that sets the pattern.

Once you establish yourself as a person of your word about adhering to a schedule, the news spreads. Speakers find they can pack into 20 minutes what they might once have taken an hour to do. (Parkinson's Law sees to that!) And committee members will love you for running a tight ship and saving them the torture of *too much talk*.

DELMONT: Another thing that drives me crazy is the presenter who comes in and goes on forever. To prevent that, we say, "You have 45 minutes, and at the end of 45 minutes we're going to excuse you if you're not done. We don't mean to be rude, but we're going to be rude. After all, we have people coming from all over the country, all over the world, so we have to stick to the agenda."

According to the U.S. Census Bureau, by the year 2000 "more than 23 million people, approximately 20 percent of the U.S. work force, will work in jobs that require narrow, special expertise . . . [not including] blue-collar workers and managers who specialize in specific fields."

Margaret Kaeter
The Age of the Specialized Generalist

CATCHING THE HARD-TO-GET SPECIALISTS

Fat also gathers when SMEs sit and sit, like prospective jurors waiting to be called. What a waste! Prisoners themselves, they're captives of the great white-collar crime.

Whenever you can exercise the influence, limit the size of a task force to a core team, usually the fewer the better. Then call on experts and representatives from potentially affected constituencies to give testimony about specific matters. Issue periodic reports to keep the voyeuristic JIC-Ps at bay and recall certain presenters as the core team makes discoveries and needs additional data. Result? Presentations that are more focused and substantive because the meeting takes on the air of a congressional hearing, rather than a exercise in transcendental meditation or a tailgate picnic at the Army-Navy game.

That's not to say there isn't a time and place for chicken and tater salad in a laid-back, carefree environment—after all, some of the best collaboration occurs then—but such events should be part of a balanced diet, not a daily regimen.

DID IT *REALLY* HELP?

Besides, or in place of, summaries from a chief listener or questions on index cards, you may want to evaluate presentations in more formal ways. Whichever your prefer, do so with these objectives:

- Check to see that the speaker's message has been clearly understood by as many on the committee as possible—ideally, everyone.

- Give less reticent participants opportunities to verbalize and clarify in ways comfortable to them.

- Help the speaker assess what worked well in the presentation and, if necessary, where further work might be done to prevent misconceptions, gaps in understandings, and the distortions of "Gossip."

In situations where you have back-to-back speakers, the evaluation sheet on page 175 can be filled out in five minutes or so after a person completes a presentation. Sharing the feedback is critical, especially for a speaker needing a 9-1-1 rescue.

Keep in mind, however, these points made by Mark Sanborn in his book, *Teambuilt*: "Criticism focuses on the person. Feedback focuses on the performance. Making me feel bad about who I am will not help me improve what I do."

15

spinning plates, swooping crows

Guiding a task force in the time-saving, pain-free writing of its final report

Group writing is an oxymoron. It's an unnatural act, or at least as difficult as what those plate spinners do for Vegas-show warmups. The challenges are tricky but exciting. Ideally, the result is a document that helps foster alignment directly or indirectly, that puts everyone on the same wavelength of understanding, heading in the same direction, planning and implementing actions consistent with the organization's mission and vision.

The document might be a business plan or a go-get-em stemwinder for the CEO. Or a marketing plan, a product rollout, an ad campaign. A request for proposal or quote, a response to one. The findings of a task force. A policy, a practice, a procedure.

No matter what they're called, how many different types there are, or the methods by which they're transmitted, too many documents are too long and broad, too jumbled and fuzzy. At best they get skimmed. At worst they're unread. None, however, is created in a vacuum. Each has its birth in a series of meetings, often reflecting the chaos from which it springs.

THE HURDLES

Writing an appealing document is hard enough for an individual. When a group attempts the task, the challenge reaches plate-spinner magnitude, especially when the direction of an organization hinges on the extent to which a document gets read and implemented. All plates must be whirl at once; none must fall.

Besides the challenge of finding exactly the right word for exactly the right place and meaning, these other hurdles are apt to line the path of a group trying to play author:

- People talk too much before getting anything on screen or paper, waiting till the last minute to meet a deadline with hastily written text. They don't realize that doodling around with sketches and copy as early as possible speeds and achieves insights they need to gain as collaborators before they can expect to communicate their shared understandings clearly and concisely.

> "They used to have a fish on the menu . . . that was smoked, grilled, *and* peppered. . . . They did everything to this fish but pistol-whip it and dress it in Bermuda shorts."
>
> *William E. Geist*
> *Food Critic*

- The group tends to view writing as stenography, not discovery. Impatient with the process and eager to get on with other things, they short-shrift the steps necessary to a worthy product—one that aids alignment.

- If they're not careful, group members may tend to make the document self-serving, of little value to others. Though the committee may have compiled alps of details, revealing specifics are not selected and arranged to deliver a dominant message everyone can understand.

- Too much attention is spent on fonts and format as well as this question: *How are we on the committee going to look?* The overriding concern should be: *How can we deliver the precise message we wish to send our audience so we can virtually guarantee it will be read, comprehended exactly as we intended, and acted upon appropriately?*

- Finally, and perhaps most counterproductive, is the group's lack of agreement on how to approach the task of producing the document. Haphazard stabs layer the slabs of fat, as committee members tap-dance to avoid writing—but salivate at the prospect of editing a colleague's draft like crows pecking at road kill.

THE PROCESS

Producing a document energizes a group, for everyone gets pleasure out of making something. (Even the snarliest of creatures would have to admit that.) Time and again I find that when a task force or similar group meets to produce a document as their "final deliverable," many of the lamented difficulties about running a meeting disappear. Here's why:

- Members see themselves accomplishing something—something tangible they can literally get their hands on.

- The process calls for "sharing space," a collective energizer.

- Individuals are collaborating, not just exchanging information.

- If the group is constantly made aware of the awaiting audience and the document's purpose, the anticipation of readership as well as the potential impact on the organization and customer become driving and unifying forces.

- Troublemakers whose behaviors were once triggered by boredom, lack of direction, or a sense of worthlessness now find they have something more interesting and constructive to do than sit, moan, and complain.

- As the document begins to grow and take shape, concerns about turf fade into the background—some slowly, some quickly—depending on how deep the emotional attachments are rooted.

- Laughter, animated talk, and queries about "What's next?" and "How may I help you?" fill an atmosphere of industry. If there's a sense of urgency, it contributes to the esprit de corps as well.

- Pride of ownership becomes imbued in the product. There's a psychological high, a genuine sense of empowerment.

THANKS, JOHN HANCOCK

Many of these outcomes can be ensured by including a signature page at the beginning of a document. Showing the participants' names, titles, and departments (if needed for credibility, leverage, or both), the page becomes a stimulator, a motivator. And it is signed according to a clause the group includes in its ground rules. For example, to ensure nobody has a change of heart about a team's decision when a boss or associate growls, "Why did you ever go for that!" a ground rule might be: *We agree to sign a report and commit to it before adjourning the meeting in which the report is completed.*

The power of the page is both subtle and significant. Not only does it help to create a more productive climate but it also prevents or discourages certain members from hiding in anonymity. That's when it's easy—and certainly no act of bravery—to be negative, surly, recalcitrant. In fact, it even makes it easier to bad-mouth a document later on if it seems politically expedient to do so. But when committee members know a signature page lies at the end of the road, with the sunlight of exposure piercing the shadows of namelessness, behaviors take on a more positive bent. It's an intriguing phenomenon.

Moreover, once the page gets instituted in the process of document-making, delegators begin to think twice about appointing warm bodies or gulag prisoners to a task force. So another major block to ineffective meetings is gradually eroded.

"But I might get a lot of calls," some will protest, particularly the chicken-hearted and politicos. "That's true," you can answer, "but if you help produce a document that's clear and beneficial to its readers, well reasoned, and consistent with the company vision, then you have little or nothing to worry about." And that's the quality of document the group should aim to achieve. Besides, if members of a task force haven't the gumption to stand behind what they write—assuming it's what they've agreed and committed to—what's the purpose of writing, and spending all that time, after all?

NO ROCKS, PLEASE

To ensure that a task force isn't expected to play ESP with either a delegator or a delegating body, such as an executive board, be sure all parties share a common, initial understanding of the intent and scope of the deliverable. There's nothing more frustrating and time-consuming than responding to the

Sisyphean taunt of "Bring Me a Rock." With each attempt (each draft), it rolls back down the hill again as the delegator complains, "It's too big. . . . It's too small. . . . It's not the right shape. . . . It's not the right texture." And even when it is the right size, shape, and texture, it isn't the right color!

What has to be realized is this: A delegator, picturing an unwritten document in the abstract, will not make the discoveries a task force makes in its collaboration. Furthermore, the group's discoveries usually won't coincide exactly with what the delegator and the team set out to do. Therefore, it's extremely important for all involved to start with a common objective about what is and is *not* to be covered by the group's work, and for you, as leader, to hold the group unflaggingly accountable to the paramount objective of the task force and why it was assembled.

HEY, REMEMBER ME!

Tattoo on the brains of committee members what the intended reader of the document is challenging them to do. I find, for example, that posting in clear sight the boldface advice on page 183—preferably atop a storyboard—serves as a constant reminder that helps melt the mountains of meeting blubber:

EYEBALLING THE BASICS, THE PERCHES

This section and the next explain how to handle the stunt of group writing, plate by spinning plate. The secret is to stick to a "process," even if you adapt the steps to online application. Participants, you will find, take quickly to the procedures, developing an ease and familiarity that will smooth the transition to more intricate and demanding electronic communications media. Here, however, the steps assume people are most comfortable and familiar with the tools cited—a solid assumption based on recent studies and, in all likelihood, bolstered by proof aplenty in your own organization.

In reading on, bear in mind that although the number of options and steps may look daunting, they're really not. They're aimed at ensuring clarity while providing a backup platter or two if any should happen to shatter. What follows immediately are the perches—the equipment and basic processes—that support the plates once they're spun into motion. Though geared to a task force, they can also be adjusted to serve any kind of committee or group.

ADVICE FROM A PROSPECTIVE READER

- **Make me care.** Tell me why I should buy into what the team has agreed to. Most important, stress the benefits to our business and customers.

- **Play prosecutor.** Build your case, so I'll deliver "the verdict" you seek.

- **Remember: I wasn't there.** I can't bring the meaning to the screen or page as well as can those who participated in the meeting.

- **Get to the bottom line.** Don't pussyfoot or fiddle-faddle. Put recommendations right up front. I'm as busy as you. I don't have time to wallow in puddings of copy. **Be brief.** But don't do it at the sacrifice of my understanding. Put only the meat of your message in the body. Shove trimmings into an appendix.

- **Thump your main points.** Make sure I hear your key messages loudly, clearly and, if necessary, repeated in different ways.

- **Give examples.** Besides verbal illustrations, I also mean schematics and matrices. The latter are particularly effective because they allow me to see interrelationships and grasp a bundle of information in one fell swoop.

- **Annotate those illustrations.** Yes indeed: A picture is worth a thousand words. But for heaven's sake, don't just plop it. Caption it!

- **Plug up the loopholes.** Care about the precision of what you write. Don't leave copy open to interpretation. I don't want *my* days flooded with e-mails, voice mails, and great waves of meetings overwhelming me with whys and what-abouts.

- **Show your conviction and enthusiasm.** They'll convince me too.

Equipment and Materials

- workstation for the recorder/publisher—computer, high-speed laser printer, high-speed copier

- laptops supplied by individuals who have them

- blank diskettes

- an extension cord or two with surge protectors

- overhead projectors, preferably two, so suggestions for changes in copy can be quickly compared, and "illustrated dialogues" can be carried on during collaboration

- one or two overhead screens

  Note: You may want to consider an LCD panel, but only if people can view projected copy without huddling and squinting, only if people see sizable chunks of copy at once, and only if the keying in of changes can be fast and nearly flawless without agonizing impatient participants held captive as they watch mistyping, backspacing, retyping, and who knows what else.

- reams of paper for the printer and copier

- 5 × 8 index cards, white and assorted colors

- 3 × 5 index cards or Post-its

- pushpins or masking tape for posting the cards

- paper clips

- write-on transparencies—plenty of them

- transparencies for printers and copiers

- fine-point transparency pens; several in black, plus assorted colors

- easel markers in assorted colors

  If you don't have every item, don't worry. There's more than one way to squeeze a tea bag. It's too easy a cop-out to say "Oh, I can't get those! Or to guffaw, "A workstation? We can hardly get an easel around here!" No matter the words, we've all sought refuge in sticking to the same old lumbering, inefficient, sit-and-nitpick ways. Just the thought of the crows and carrion should give us sufficient reason to shout, "We've been there, done that, and don't want to do it again!"

Up to the Starting Point

Steps like these can help bring a group to the point of writing. They reflect a high-level overview of a collaborative get-together running a couple of days or longer:

1. The leader calls the meeting to order, reviews the objectives on the overhead, reminds the group of the ground rules they had established weeks earlier.

2. The group debates the objectives and alters some of the wording, which is subsequently endorsed by the sponsoring manager.

3. Each item on the agenda is deliberated—at times heatedly—with the leader playing her or his various roles and keeping the discourse moving with the "follow-the-thread" technique plus index-card responses, handouts, and procedure maps that get participants interacting on the shared space of overhead transparencies, copyboard illustrations, and the like.

4. At appropriate times, participants add notes for tasks, issues, and such to the posted easel sheets, based on discoveries they make among themselves by debating the issues, accomplishing the tasks, gaining insights from presentations by subject-matter experts, and so on. Meanwhile, depending on which choices they make from those described below, they "divide and conquer" the writing of their final report.

To Divide and Conquer

Distributing responsibilities for drafting and revising not only gets the work done quicker but, in a way, seduces participants into creating and collaborating. Following are some options:

• **Plan for big blocks of time during the meeting** when people can, for example, return to their workstations for breakouts or work with laptops in the meeting room.

  Note: In settings where it's not possible to have a recorder/publisher with workstation, this may be the only option around which to build the activity.

• **Allow certain members to go offline to write** while other members conduct business that doesn't require the attention of the writers or can be summarized for them later on.

• **Adjourn early after "homework assignments" have been given.**

• **Invite one member to create a jump-start draft** and then, depending on the quality of the document, decide if the person should continue as the sole writer working with feedback from the group or whether the group should assume the task. (For either approach, see "Pulling It Off!" later in this chapter.)

- **Elicit suggestions** from the group.

- **Whenever helpful, provide templates** to assist less competent writers and ensure consistency where necessary.

A recorder/publisher can also help divide and conquer. His or her task should be to:

- **Produce and track a master copy** by either keying in hard copy the writers submit or transferring soft copy from the files on their individual diskettes.

- **Make transparencies** of the pages with a high-speed laser printer.

- **Run off sets of hard copy** as needed, or signal a runner to perform the task.

Note: If assignments are taken as homework, you might require each writer to make his or her own sets of hard copy and transparencies. If you do, be sure the recorder/publisher is kept in sync.

PHILLIPS: "Divide and conquer" in writing a group report can significantly reduce the time to meet a team's objectives. However, you can avoid inconsistent styles and content in the team's deliverable by not dividing into more than two or three subgroups.

The "Official Version" of a Draft

Let a set of transparencies tracked by you and the recorder/publisher become the "official version" that's revised and edited. By directing the group's attention to the screen, all members see exactly what is being inserted and deleted, so they don't waste time just following hard copy and imploring: "Where are you now? Run that by me again. Say that once more, I'm confused." That approach leads to water torture and conflicting versions of a revised draft.

To Speed Feedback and Revision

During the process, make sure, perhaps with a handout or on-screen template, that anyone producing copy does the following, either independently or with the help of the recorder/publisher:

1. Number the pages and *the lines of text at the left* for speeding citations during feedback and revision.

2. Double-space the copy for interlinear editing.

3. Make a transparency of each page as the "official version" of the draft.

4. Get hard copy made and distributed so committee members always have a complete, up-to-date draft for reference.

Overall Steps for Critiquing and Revising

When the time comes, have each writer do the following, starting with the first page demanding revision.

1. Work with the "official version" transparencies, projecting each on the screen for group feedback, expedited by citing line numbers.

2. Conduct an initial sweep of the copy, limiting suggestions to content only, i.e., the messages that grow out of the group's collaboration. On the transparency, make marginal notes for significant changes. If helpful, also jot down interlinear suggestions, but beware the caws and cackles. *Note:* You may find it a boon, as I have, to place the following definition on a sign posted at the base of the overhead projector:

   SWEEP: Give a writer substantive suggestions for revising copy without picking flyspecks from pepper.

   Some crows require months of training and restraint.

3. Revise, acting on the suggested changes.

4. Conduct a second sweep and, if necessary, a third.

5. Do a final edit, following the process outlined in "Pulling It Off."

For Feedback From an Individual

When an individual wants to suggest a revision, she or he should:

1. Cite the pertinent line number(s).

2. Tell what she or he wants to change and why, focusing on the accuracy of the message, the potential response of the reader(s), or both.

3. Do *one* of the following if the proposed change runs three lines or more:

   —Prepare a transparency well ahead of time, perhaps while studying the document during an overnight reading period. Then display the revision, when the time comes, on a second projector so the differences between the original and revised copy can be readily discerned.

   —Take the preceding step but with a transparency prepared on the spot.

   —Put a blank transparency over the "official version," pen in the changes, and paper-clip the two.

   Note: A handout or template of the preceding steps might also be prepared and distributed.

PULLING IT OFF!

To whirl the plates—to guide the meeting participants in creating and polishing a draft while appealing to a range of personalities, perspectives, expectations, and language abilities, not to mention the business drivers, the customer, and the need for alignment—take these tips. (Phew! Quite a few plates to spin.) Like all previous suggestions, these, too, can be either cherry-picked or adjusted for groups of various sizes and differing objectives.

> **SUNDY: Out of an experiment or series of experiments may come a table or pictures of something. And that's usually where I start in writing a paper; I'll put the illustrative material together first. . . . In the end, I hope there'll be enough strong data to prove the hypothesis—or disprove it—with a narrative to support the outcome. Most researchers think first in terms of pictures and tables, even though the approach and the hypothesis may ultimately change.**

If You Begin With a Jump-Start Document . . .

1. Invite someone to produce a draft, including, if possible, a pivotal schematic. Enlist a committee member whose emotional attachment to the draft can be subordinated to his or her desire to get things off center, to start debate, to make progress.

2. Give the group time to read hard copy of the draft.

3. Conduct an initial sweep in answer to this question: *In terms of our audience and purpose, is the draft worth working with? Why or why not?* If the draft misses target, scrap it! Too many groups try to salvage a disaster or an inappropriate piece with line-by-line editing. It's foolish—and often impossible.

   If the draft is "almost there," have the writer:

1. Conduct an initial sweep in answer to these questions, which might also be made into a handout, a poster, or a transparency shown with the second projector:

   • How well has the case been built?
   • Is the dominant message coming through? Why or why not?
   • If you were a prospective reader, how might you respond? Why?
   • Also, as surrogate reader, would you get lost anywhere? If so, where and why?

2. Proceed with other business, after agreeing with the writer about a deadline for the revision, which he or she might perform offline and perhaps right then.

3. Conduct a second sweep and, in most cases, go immediately into final editing, following the steps outlined on pages 190–192.

   If the draft shows promise but needs a healthy revision, have the group agree on how they prefer to divide and conquer. Then:

1. Do an initial sweep of the parts needing revision, with each reviser of a part seeking answers to the four questions above.

2. Revise (by the divide-and-conquer method the group chooses).

3. Do a second sweep and, if necessary, a third.

4. Conduct a final edit.

If You Start With a Storyboard . . .

1. Lay out a tentative flow for a draft, using 5 × 8 index (topic) cards of different colors or white cards with different color lettering to indicate segments of the eventual document.

2. Readjust the sequence to accommodate discoveries made during deliberation. *Note:* Have the recorder/publisher keep abreast of inputting changes to the storyboard's parallel so he or she can provide a printout to each group member when it's time to divide and conquer. Also, to help prospective writers listen more acutely and take better memory-jogging notes about deliberations on segments of the proposed document, assign segments for which each writer will be ultimately responsible. Put their initials on the appropriate topic cards.

3. Use 3 × 5 index cards or Post-its to make notes about supporting details for each topic card, and post them in a kite's tail below it. Or as the meeting progresses, simply pen in notes on the 5 × 8 cards or ask a volunteer to do so.

4. Divide and conquer, using a previously cited method above.

5. Proceed with sweeps and a final edit.

To Do the Final Edit, Including Copy Editing

Either you, as editor in chief, or someone appointed to the position, should:

1. Have hard copies of the document made for everyone. Also have one master set of transparencies made as the "official version."

2. Before the group assembles, post an easel sheet of items the recorder/publisher—as well as you or a selected member of the group—will ultimately tend to as "global edits." They are complete searches of a manuscript for specific items that would customarily be the purview of a copy editor, proofreader, or both. For example:

For Global Edits, we will . . .

- do a spellcheck
- change "client" to "Techno•Logical"
- change "we" to "task force"
- hyphenate "first-time use"

3. Also before the group convenes, make an Edit-Tracker by posting two or three easel sheets, each with these headings and columns:

PAGE	PERSON	LINE(S)

4. Allow the group time to read and mark up the complete document, which, by this time, usually doesn't demand a CAT scan.

After the group has finished reading and marking:

5. Elicit suggestions for additions to the global edits.

6. Conduct a flip-through of the entire document, which, in most cases, shouldn't take more than 10 or 15 minutes. During the flip-through, people who wish to speak about certain pages and lines should raise their hands and, when called on, indicate which lines they intend to address. Ask a committee member or the recorder/publisher—or even a JIC-P!—to log in the citations. For example:

> ". . . Hews of North Carolina, a consistent voter against the Declaration, started suddenly upright, and lifting up both his Hands to Heaven as if he had been in a trance, cry'd out, 'It is done! and I will abide by it.'"
>
> *Fawn M. Brodie*
> Thomas Jefferson: An Intimate History

PAGE	PERSON	LINE(S)
4	LC	2–4
9	BP	7, 9
	RM	15–23
17	LC	8

Note: When the flip-through is completed, group members usually find they already agree on most of the content, a fact that cannot be quickly determined if pages are either hopscotched or gone through front to back without the initial assessment. Also, absent a preview that reveals the degree of consensus, a concern about an early page—or one pounced on by an intimidator or saboteur—can turn into heated debate at a poorly run meeting. The turmoil then leads people to conclude erroneously that the entire document is a sinking trawler, leaving you a drowning captain in a frenzy of tiger sharks. Finally, the Edit-Tracker helps people size up what lies ahead, encouraging them to be more selective and concise with their comments.

7. Proceed with the citations on the Edit-Tracker by doing the following:
   - Project the first requested page from the "official version."
   - Dealing with the tagged lines in sequence (starting with lines 2 to 4 in the previous sample), pen in the suggested changes, either directly on the "official version" transparency or on an overlay of it. If the overlay revision is approved by the group, or if someone's prepared revision is accepted instead, paper-clip the final, approved revision to its original, counterpart transparency.
   - Cross off each citation after addressing the related matter.

PAGE	PERSON	LINE(S)
~~4~~	~~LC~~	~~2-4~~
9	BP	7, 9

Note: After their work has been completed, have members pen the signature page before adjourning (if that was their agreement), since the rest of the procedure deals with tidying up the piece and doesn't involve them. If, however, the group prefers to convene for one last look, it must be done to check the accuracy of the copyediting only. Do not allow anyone—potentially a wishy-washy individual who has had second thoughts prompted by a bully of a boss in the background—to reopen Pandora's Box by discussing the decision itself. Pandora can deal a deathly blow.

8. Meet with the recorder/publisher to transfer and double-check changes from the transparencies to the master disk. Tend to the global edits.

9. Publish and distribute the document.

10. Savor the delights of a tough job well done. Congratulate yourself for keeping the crows at bay. Then, still basking in the afterglow, pack your plates for the next occasion.

THE REWARDS

Believe it or not, you'll look forward to that next time. As mountain climber Stevie Haston says, "If I do a bolt route, it's nice, but the memory is short. If I climb a hard alpine route, the memory lasts forever."

That's how exhilarating the meeting process can also be, when it's uncluttered and fat-free. Then the essence of a legitimate challenge—with its yeast of tug and thrust, fun and excitement—can bring pleasure and immense satisfaction, not only to those of us who meet to do business but to the customers we serve.

a final toast

"The qualities of an exceptional cook," food critic Bryan Miller reminds us, "are akin to those of a successful tight-rope walker: an abiding passion for the task, courage to go out on a limb, and an impeccable sense of balance."

Bon Appetit!

NOTES

part I

11 "This process is used mainly": Irma S. Rombauer and Marion Rombauer Becker, *Joy of Cooking* (New York: Scribner, 1995), p. 154.

CHAPTER 1

4 Research by George Stalk and Tom Hout: Oren Harari, "Why Don't Things Change?," *Management Review* (February 1995), p. 32.

4 "Netscape is like a rocket": Patricia Sellers, "What Exactly Is Charisma?" *Fortune* (January 15, 1996), p. 71.

4 What's more, 91 percent never return: Michael LeBoeuf, *How to Win Customers and Keep Them for Life* (New York: Berkley Books, 1987), p. 13.

5 "If an organization isn't generating": Tom McDonald, "Brain Trust," *Successful Meetings* (January 1995), p. 16.

5 "Soft skills are every bit": Connie Bovier, "Teamwork: The Heart of an Airline," *Training* (June 1993), p. 55.

5 rise of teams in nearly 73 percent of U.S. businesses: Robert Carey, "Team Playing," *Successful Meetings* (March 1995), p. 92.

5 while in Fortune 500 companies: Samuel Greengard citing a statistic from the Center for Workforce Effectiveness in "Making the Virtual Office a Reality," *Personnel Journal* (September 1994), p. 71.

5 "most managers have absolutely no training": Virginia Johnson, "Budget Cuts," *Successful Meetings* (March 1991), p. 124.

6 Not just because networks of telecommuters: Samuel Greengard citing a statistic from the Telecommuting Advisory Council in "Making the Virtual Office a Reality," *Personnel Journal* (September 1994), p. 71.

6 most employees spend between 50 percent and 80 percent of their time in meetings: Tom McDonald, "The Think System," *Successful Meetings* (February 1995), p. 26.

6 "*Industry Week* has referred to the $37 billion wasted annually": John Sheridan, "A $37 Billion Waste," *Industry Week* (September 4, 1989), pp. 11–12.

6 "training in how to manage meetings": "Brilliant Meetings: The Art of Effective Visual Presentations," (Austin, TX: 3M Meeting Management Institute, 1995), p. 1.

6 "Not everything counts": Charles Garfield, *Peak Performers: The New Heroes of American Business* (New York: Avon Books, 1986), p. 156.

7 "30 percent to 50 percent of [the] meetings that fail": Michael Lee Smith, "Conducting a Meeting," *Supervisory Management* (March 1995), p. 7.

7 the get-togethers where one-fourth of the participants say they discuss irrelevant issues: Peter R. Monge, Charles McSween, and JoAnne Wyer, "A Profile of

Meetings in America: Results of the 3M Meeting Effectiveness Study" [Annenberg School of Communications, University of Southern California, Los Angeles, CA, November 1989], *Research Registry* (Austin, Texas: 3M Meeting Management Institute, 1993), unpaged.

7   and a third feel they have little or no influence on the outcomes anyway: *Research Registry,* ibid, unpaged.

7   "$170 billion annually—12 percent of the payroll": Kate Ludeman, "Bosses, Embrace Your Workers!" *The New York Times,* May 14, 1989, p. C2.

7   "at a 21 percent annual clip since 1989": Richard Moody, "Talking Through Wires," *Successful Meetings* (February 1995), p. 118.

7   With companies reorganizing on an average of every 18 months: Virginia Johnson, "Taking Risks," *Successful Meetings* (November 1992), p. 113.

8   "is ten times more important to profitability": Gary Fellers, *Why Things Go Wrong: Deming Philosophy in a Dozen Ten-Minute Sessions* (Gretna, Louisiana: Pelican Publishing Conpany, 1994), p. 18.

CHAPTER 2

11   "The more technology you have in your office": Ross Weiland, "2001: A Meetings Odyssey," *Successful Meetings* (December 1993), p. 34.

12   "Collaboration . . . is the process of *shared creation*": Michael Schrage, *No More Teams! Mastering the Dynamics of Creative Collaboration* (New York: Currency/ Doubleday, 1995), p. 33.

12   "In practice . . . collaboration is a far richer process": ibid., p. 32.

12   "In the beginning was the word": *Holy Bible,* John 1: 1.

CHAPTER 3

16   "Work expands so as to fill the time available for its completion": C. Horthocote Parkinson (Boston: Houghton Mifflin Company, 1957), p. 2.

23   His behavior bore out: Wharton Research Center: 3M Meeting Management Team, *How to Run Better Business Meetings* (New York: McGraw-Hill Book Company, 1987), pp. 108–114.

23   "To explain himself": Noel Tichy and Stratford Sherman, *Control Your Destiny or Someone Else Will* (New York: HarperCollins, 1994), p. 11.

24   "The English language is built on *polar terms*": Richard C. Maybury, "Principles of Sending Clear and Uncontaminated Messages," *Using Dialogue and Discussion* (Work in Progress, 1996), pp. 68–69. I am indebted to Maybury for his contributions to this topic.

24   "With this in mind": ibid.

CHAPTER 4

31   "122 million meals served": Anita Pyzik Lienert, "From Moving Tanks to Moving Merchandise," *Management Review* (June 1994), p. 30.

31   "6000-employee operation": ibid.

32 "Yes, I have been using 3×5 cards at Sears": William G. Pagonis (personal communication, September 14, 1995).

34 "are too ephemeral to be effective": William G. Pagonis, *Moving Mountains: Lessons in Leadership and Logistics from the Gulf War* (Boston: Harvard Business School Press, 1992), p. 190.

35 "An Indian mongoose": *Reader's Digest Exploring the Secrets of Nature* (London: The Reader's Digest Association Limited, 1994), p. 291.

CHAPTER 5

45 Pull the plug on the company's e-mail system: Charles B. Wang (personal communication, February 6, 1996).

CHAPTER 6

65 "People don't like distance": Virginia Johnson, "Two-Person Interactions: Trifle or Treasure?," *Successful Meetings* (December 1992), p. 129.

65 "where people talk": Michael A. Cusumano and Richard W. Selby, *Microsoft Secrets: How the World's Most Powerful Software Company Creates Technology, Shapes Markets, and Manages People* (New York: The Free Press, 1995), p. 343.

65 Similarly, program managers hold "blue tray" lunches: ibid., p. 344.

66 "One of the things": Herman Cain, *The Hour of Power* television broadcast, March 17, 1996.

part II

67 "No restaurant can run successfully without teamwork": Charlie Trotter, *Charlie Trotter's* (Berkeley, CA: Ten Speed Press, 1994), p. 13.

CHAPTER 7

72 "The beginning is the most important": Plato [The Republic. Book II] quoted in John Bartlett, *Familiar Quotations,* 11th Edition (Boston: Little Brown and Company, 1938), p. 973.

74 "If I have seen further": Sir Isaac Newton quoted in Louis E. Boone, *Quotable Business* (New York: Random House, 1992), p. 25.

76 "If you refuse to accept anything but the best": Somerset Maugham quoted in ibid, p. 133.

84 ". . . I feel that the two rhythms": Sidney Gottlieb, ed., *Hitchcock on Hitchcock: Selected Writings and Interviews* (Berkeley, CA: University of California Press, 1995), p. 269.

86 "He who laughs, lasts": Robert Fulghum quoted in Louis E. Boone, op. cit., p. 247.

86 "The secret of happiness": James Barrie quoted in Louis E. Boone, op. cit., 248.

CHAPTER 8

89 "If a house be divided against itself": *Holy Bible,* Mark 3:25.

91   preferably four to seven members: Glenn M. Parker, "Cross-Functional Collaboration," *Training and Development* (October 1994), p. 53.

103   "What a person really fears": Ernest Becker, *The Denial of Death* (New York: The Free Press, 1973), p. 153.

104   "cannot make a decision": Theodore Isaac Rubin, *Overcoming Indecisiveness: The Eight Stages of Effective Decision-Making* (Avon Books, 1985), pp. 15–16.

104   "Provide introverts with an agenda": Richard C. Maybury (personal correspondence, February 13, 1996).

110   "I can tell more about how a company's doing": Bill Fromm, *The Ten Commandments of Business—and How to Break Them* (New York, G. P. Putnam's Sons, 1991), p. 159.

part III

111   "As with many traditional French dishes": John Ayto, *The Diner's Dictionary: Food and Drink from A to Z* (New York: Oxford University Press, 1993), p. 38.

CHAPTER 10

119   "Some 80 to 90 percent of the significant features": Edward T. Hall and Mildred Reed Hall, *Hidden Differences: Doing Business with the Japanese* (New York: Anchor Books, 1989), p. xvii.

127   "A problem well stated": Charles Kettering quoted in Boone, op. cit., p. 85.

CHAPTER 11

137   "Remember the Big Fact!": Rubin, op. cit., p. 134.

CHAPTER 12

138   "If in doubt, have a handout": David A. Peoples, *Presentations Plus*, 2d Edition (New York: John Wiley & Sons, 1992), p. 105.

CHAPTER 13

152   "It takes shared space to create shared understandings": Schrage, op. cit., p. 223.

159   "People sometimes talk of me": Thomas Edison quoted in James D. Newton, *Uncommon Friends* (New York: Harcourt, Brace Jovanovich, 1987), p. 18.

159   "We do not write in order to be understood": C. Day Lewis quoted in Donald M. Murray, *Shoptalk: Learning to Write with Writers* (Portsmouth, NH: Boynton/Cook Publishers, 1990), p. 6.

162   "Manhattan is a narrow island": Raymond Sokolov quoted in James B. Simpson, comp., *Simpson's Contemporary Quotations* (Boston: Houghton Mifflin Company, 1988), p. 300.

CHAPTER 14

164 "the Victorian principle of furnishing": Charles Kuralt, *Charles Kuralt's America* (New York: G. P. Putnam's Sons, 1995), p. 55.

168 "The best way to be boring": Voltaire quoted in Boone, op. cit., p. 70.

168 "can actually process visuals 60,000 times faster than text": "Brilliant Meetings," op. cit., p. 12.

176 "According to the U.S. Census Bureau": Margaret Kaeter, "The Age of the Specialized Generalist," *Training* (December 1993), p. 50.

177 "Criticism focuses on the person": Mark Sanborn, *Teambuilt* (New York: MasterMedia Limited, 1994) p. 143.

CHAPTER 15

179 "They used to have a fish on the menu": William E. Geist, "Hail, Cholesterol: Beefeaters End Years of Guilt," *The New York Times*, March 28, 1987, p. 29.

191 ". . . Hews of North Carolina": Fawn M. Brodie, *Thomas Jefferson: An Intimate History* (New York: W. W. Norton & Company, Inc., 1974), p. 123.

193 "If I do a bolt route": Stevie Haston, "The Bad Brit," *Rock & Ice* (September/October 1995), p. 56.

A Final Toast

194 "The qualities of an exceptional cook": Bryan Miller, "What Makes a Great Cook Great," *The New York Times*, February 23, 1983, p. C1.

Kudos for Fat Free Meetings

This book is right on target and will do more for productivity than rightsizing, restructuring, TQM, and all the other management quick fixes.
Buck Rogers
former Vice President, Worldwide Marketing, IBM
and author of *The IBM Way*

I loved the book! It is so much more than a book about meetings. It's about people communicating, working as a team, and most importantly, treating people with respect. Delightful reading, it's a must-have for everyone.
Linda A. Holbrook
General Manager
Vanguard Communications Corporation

Pointless meetings cost millions . . . Albert shows tested ways to cut through the fog and make meetings productive.
R. S. Harrah
Project Development Engineer
Stewart & Stevenson Services

Burt Albert is an incredibly amusing and energetic writer who's turned a potentially dull subject into a fast-paced and—believe it or not—very entertaining page-turner. Chock-full of dynamite ideas, his provocatively insightful book should become the procedures manual in every organization committed to serving its demanding customers—the ultimate goal Albert never lets meeting-goers forget. He's clear, colorful, and compelling!
Elaine Haglund, Ph.D.
Professor, Educational Psychology, and Director
International Academic Projects
California State University, Long Beach

An essential guide through the maze of the meeting minefield. Pragmatic solutions to every obstacle that does or could arise.
J. Byron Davies
Vice President, Investments
Advest, Inc.

INDEX

index

index

Broaden Your Thinking & Sharpen Your Management Skills

Cultural Diversity Fieldbook
George F. Simons, Bob Abramms & L. Ann Hopkins, with Diane J. Johnson
For discovery, discussion, and action—leading thought and best practices from a wide array of specialists. Over 100 interviews, articles, essays, and poems from some of today's most prominent business leaders and publications. Helps you deal effectively with issues such as affirmative action, sensitizing workforces, and corporate diversity programs.
ISBN 1-56079-602-2, 272 pp., 8 x 8, $26.95 pb

Business Briefs
165 Guiding Principles From the World's Sharpest Minds
Russ Wild
You will benefit from this collection of 165 short, pithy pieces of career and business advice from some the world's best thinkers. Topics include networking upward, difficult bosses, business lunching, brainstorming basics, and more.
ISBN 1-56079-595-6, 192 pp., 6 x 9, $16.95 pb

21st Century Manager
Meeting the Challenges and Opportunities of the New Corporate Age
Gareth S. Gardiner
Offers practical advice to help you meet the challenges and opportunities of today's rapidly changing business community. It presents a framework for successfully managing well into the next century, offering specific approaches to a variety of management challenges.
ISBN 1-56079-455-0, 208 pp., 6 x 9, $22.95 hc

Why Change Doesn't Work
Harvey Robbins and Michael Finley
From the authors of the award-winning *Why Teams Don't Work*, this new book offers expert opinions on why companies fail in their attempts at change, and provides sound advice on how to overcome setbacks and make changes for the better.
ISBN 1-56079-675-8, 240 pp., 6 x 9, $24.95 pb

Available at Fine Bookstores Near You

Or Order Direct
Call: 800-338-3282   Fax: 609-243-915

Visit Peterson's Education Center
On the Internet
http://www.petersons.com

P Peterson's P.O. Box 2123, Princeton, NJ